The Bible and Recent Archaeology

THE
BIBLE
AND RECENT
ARCHAEOLOGY

Kathleen M. Kenyon

A Colonnade Book
published by
British Museum Publications Limited

Colonnade Books
are published by British Museum Publications Ltd,
and are offered as contributions to the enjoy-
ment, study, and understanding of art,
archaeology and history.
  The same publishers also produce the official
publications of the British Museum.

Reprinted 1979, 1985, 1986
ISBN 0 7141 8003 3 *paper*
Published by British Museum Publications Ltd
46 Bloomsbury Street, London WC1B 3QQ

Designed by Dodd and Dodd
Set in 10 on 12pt 'Compugraphic' Baskerville
Printed and bound in Great Britain by
Biddles Ltd, Guildford and King's Lynn

Contents

Introduction

The basis of this book is the text of the four Haskell lectures which I gave at Oberlin University, Ohio in 1976. I am most grateful to the Haskell Lectureship Committee and especially to Professor H. T. Frank for the opportunity to give these lectures and to visit the Oberlin campus. The lectures were given to a mixed university audience of senior and junior members and the resultant book is intended for a general readership of those interested in the Bible and its setting, and *not* for specialists, be they textual critics, historians or archaeologists.

The title chosen consciously echoes that of my father's book, *The Bible and Archaeology*, published in 1940. He had been induced to write it to place the Bible in its setting against the background of the vast increase in knowledge of the history of Western Asia that had accrued in the preceding one hundred years, and especially in the period since the end of World War I. Egypt had been relatively well known for many years, though the Tutankhamun finds had provided a brilliant highlight in the inter-War period. However, the Hittites, Crete, the Mesopotamian dynasties including that of Ur, the Hurrian kingdom of Mitanni, were all just emerging from obscurity into a firm historical picture. It had, moreover, been a period of very remarkable finds of archives, at Nuzi, Mari, Ras Shamra; Alalakh, though by 1940 only a small portion of the tablets had been interpreted.

The approach here is very different. The history of the great Empires is mainly left in the background as not requiring further description and as part of well-accepted history. The recent archaeology and new historical interpretation are based on excavations mainly carried out or at least published since the Second World War, on the publication and translation during that time of texts recovered in excavations in Syria, and on modern approaches in literary criticism of the Old Testament.

The amount of information derived from excavations in Palestine has very much increased since 1940 when only one chapter in *The Bible and Archaeology* was devoted to Palestine. Here Palestine will form a much greater part.

Finally, there is bound to be a difference in approach in that I am an archaeologist, an excavator, whereas my father was a classical scholar and an authority on the textual criticism of the New Testament. His contacts with archaeology were those of the Director of the British Museum, responsible for the archaeological objects therein and for the Museum sponsorship of excavations at Ur and Carchemish.

1 The Patriarchs and the Background to the Old Testament

It is necessary to start with some reference to the most generally accepted views of a critical approach to the Biblical texts, in this case in the Pentateuch. The literary analysis of Genesis and Exodus alone has produced almost as many theories and interpretations as there are authors. Not being a literary critic oneself, one tends to accept the interpretation which seems most reasonable, without being able to judge the linguistic and textual problems involved. It is possible, however, to set the hypotheses against the historical and archaeological evidence and see how they fit.

All reputable modern scholars accept as certain that the Pentateuch, as well as the Books of Joshua, Judges, and the others early in the sequence, only acquired the form in which they have reached us by a very long process of the combination of oral and tribal records, of editing and redactions. It is accepted that there are three main elements in the Pentateuch: the Yahwist, or J; the Elohist, or E; and the priestly, or P. The interests of J are concentrated in the south of Palestine and in Transjordan. It is probably the work of a single author, using the traditions he had collected, but there is no evidence of an earlier written source. It is suggested that the author was a Judaean in the royal household, probably in the reign of Solomon in the middle of the tenth century BC. He had collected together the tribal traditions surviving by oral transmission amongst the population which by then was well settled. The E element represents the traditions of the population settled in the north of the country. Most authorities date it to the eighth century BC, after the separation of the northern kingdom of Israel from Judah in the south. It is possible (though critics argue the point) that the E chronicler used a source in common with that used by the J chronicler. The P element is very much later, being the work of the priests of the Jerusalem Temple

about the time of the return from the Babylonian Exile, c. 530 BC. The combination of all the elements comes later. The complete canon of the Old Testament is probably not earlier than 300 BC. Among the difficulties of dealing with the results of the textual criticism is very considerable disagreement amongst the critics as to which sections are to be ascribed to which source.

These paragraphs on textual interpretation of the early books of the Old Testament have been necessary to emphasise the long distance in time separating the redaction of the Biblical record and the period of the Patriarchs, during which ancestral tribal history suffered all the vicissitudes of oral transmission that can be documented in connection with similar nomadic or semi-nomadic groups. Invented pedigrees and anachronisms play a large part in such records. It is against this understanding of the nature of the Old Testament records that we now turn to the history of Western Asia as revealed by modern archaeology which forms the background for the story of the Patriarchs.

The Genesis account describes Abraham as journeying from Ur to Haran and on to Hebron in the land of Canaan. The almost legendary nature of this account will be referred to later, and is well illustrated by the highly improbable ages ascribed to the Patriarchs. The itinerary is not an impossible one, though Ur is rather improbable, and it fringes the semi-desert of north Syria. This area was frequented by the sort of group indicated by the description of Abraham and his family as semi-nomads whose economy was based on flocks and herds of small animals, sheep and goats, not on cattle and certainly not provided with the camel of the true nomad. Northern Syria at this time provides vivid archaeological and textual evidence of competing economies. The history of the successive imperial states of Mesopotamia in the fourth and third millennia are by now well known as the result of decades of excavations. In power they were comparable with that of the Old Kingdom of Egypt. Cultural and commercial contacts between the successive Mesopotamian powers spread right across the Anatolian foothills to the Mediterranean coast, being seen, for instance, at Ras Shamra-Ugarit. Similarly, Egyptian contacts spread up the Mediterranean coast to Byblos (traditionally Gebal). Within this great arc there was a continuum of prosperous urban states, maintaining to a large degree their own individuality, but with considerable cultural unity (1). They were prepared to defend themselves against jealous neighbours by the building of strong city walls, of which Syria and Palestine provide many examples. In the third millennium BC, the Early Bronze Age, there certainly appears along the whole length of the Mediterranean coast a cultural unity, firmly shown by pottery and other objects of common use, extending from Ras Shamra-Ugarit in the north through

Byblos to the Palestinian sites of Megiddo, Beth-shan and Jericho.

Recently information has begun to emerge concerning the remarkable finds at Tell Mardikh in north Syria (2) identified as the city of Ebla. In the last centuries of the third millennium BC Ebla was the centre of a state which could rival those of Mesopotamia, and could at times subjugate them. The achievements of Ebla and the details of its administration and foreign relationships are recorded in an enormous archive of 14,000 or so tablets, of which the translation has only just begun (3). These records have a special interest for Biblical scholars, for the language is West Semitic and it is suggested that it should be called proto-Canaanite. It therefore is a very early member of the family tree of Hebrew. Names allied to those found in the accounts of the Patriarchs have been found, and the evidence from this new literature will, when the study is complete, add much to the Biblical background. It must

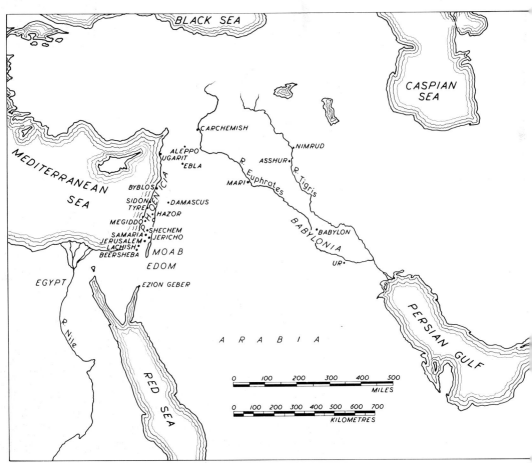

1 The Middle East before the Exodus

2 Tell Mardikh-Ebla. View of the Acropolis with the Lower City to the south, from the south-west

3 East wall of the Room of State Archives with cuneiform inscribed tablets *in situ* at Tell Mardikh-Ebla

be stressed, however, that the archive belongs to a period some four or five hundred years before the earliest dates proposed for the Patriarchs and a thousand years before the entry into Canaan.

At the end of the third millennium the comfortable civilised life of the great powers of Egypt and Mesopotamia and the city states or cities which extended up the Mediterranean coast and across the arc to the Euphrates-Tigris basin received a considerable shock. In the Mesopotamian records the disturbance to civilisation is ascribed to the Amurru, a group speaking a West Semitic language. In Egypt, the disturbances that intervened between the properous years of the Old Kingdom and the re-establishment of authority by the Twelfth Dynasty of the Middle Kingdom, are ascribed to Asiatic incursions.

It is generally accepted that it was to the Amurru or Amorite setting that the Patriarchs belong. Some authorities place them in the nineteenth to eighteenth centuries BC, on the basis of the form of their names and of the fact that Baal has not yet started to supplant El in the Canaanite pantheon. I would prefer a later date, seventeenth or sixteenth century but without strong grounds and only because I would prefer to reduce the length of period in which traditions had survived. There is no archaeological evidence, so this is only expressing a view unbacked by any form of scientific support.

It is, however, relevant to show the archaeological evidence for this Amurru intervention in civilised life, since it certainly has a bearing on the way of life of the Patriarchs. The archaeological record proves that, in sites going from north to south, at Ras Shamra-Ugarit, Byblos-Gebal, Megiddo, Jericho, Lachish, ancient Gaza, there is an absolute break. In most places there is an interruption of town life, though at Byblos and Megiddo there may be slender continuity. Perhaps I may be allowed to start with Jericho, for here I am completely confident of the exactness of the archaeological record.

The city of the Early Bronze Age at Jericho had a long life, with a very complex succession of rebuildings of the city walls. The dating of these walls depends on Egyptian chronology,

and the various shifts in this cause one some anxieties. Roughly, however, they cover the period 3000 to 2300 BC. The final wall was violently burnt (a burning erroneously ascribed by previous excavators to the period of Joshua). In the succeeding period there was a gap of which the only evidence on the town site was of camping occupation, succeeded by some rather poor buildings, quite different from what went before and what came in the succeeding Middle Bronze Age.

The gap and the period of the succeeding insignificant buildings on the town site is filled by evidence from the tombs.

In the Early Bronze Age there were cut into the rocky slopes surrounding the mound large tombs containing hundreds of burials. In the subsequent Middle Bronze Age, there were multiple successive burials, which can be interpreted as family vaults used over a number of generations. In the intervening period, in which there is a gap in town life, the tombs were completely different. For this period the designation Intermediate Early Bronze Age—Middle Bronze Age period, abbreviated EB-MB, I believe to be the most appropriate (though American and Israeli archaeologists continue to use Middle Bronze I, the designation given by Professor Albright). These tombs are utterly different from those that went before and their Middle Bronze Age successors. They are individual tombs (with a very few containing two bodies), and they exhibit a number of very well-differentiated characteristics.

The contrast between the tombs of the Early Bronze Age and of the EB-MB period can be emphasised by simple statistics. In the 1952-8 excavations, nine Early Bronze Age tombs were cleared. The estimated number of individuals buried is 469. For the EB-MB period, 346 tombs were cleared, and the estimated number of individuals is 356. These figures high-light the contrast between the mass burial chambers of the Early Bronze Age, with up to 89 bodies in a single tomb, and the enormous proliferation of tomb chambers, almost all with a single body, a few with two, and one with three.

Another feature of interest in the EB-MB tombs was differences of burial practices within the group. The tombs of the first group were called Dagger Tombs, since the characteristic

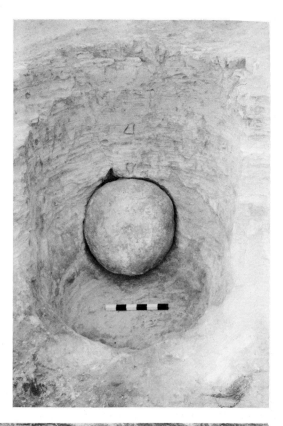

4, 5 *Right*, the shaft of a Dagger Tomb at Jericho with a boulder sealing the entrance to the chamber. *Below*, an intact burial with a characteristic bronze dagger beside the skeleton

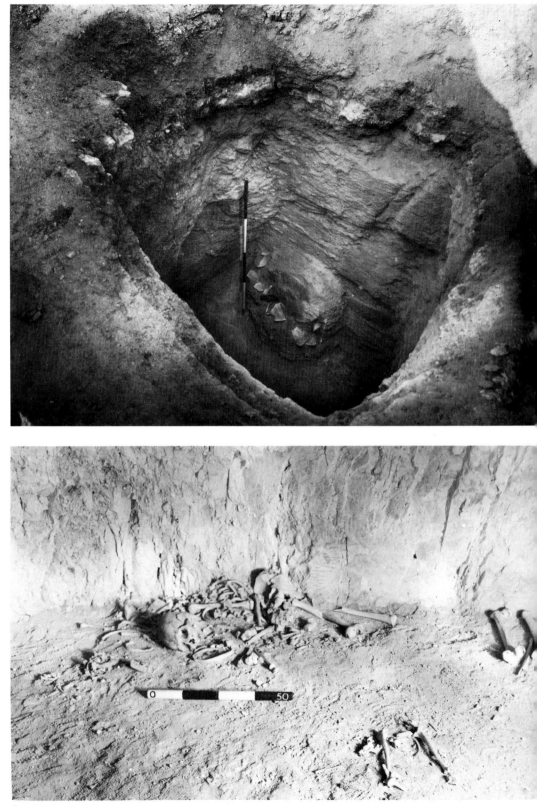

grave offering was a single dagger; some burials were accompanied only by beads, and these individuals may be identified as women. The tombs of this group were characterised by a small, neat shaft, only about one metre deep (4), and a small neat chamber. In them the intact body was laid in a crouched position (5).

The tombs of the second group identified were given the name Pottery Tombs, since they contained no weapons but groups of little jars, and usually a single four-spouted lamp placed in a niche. The technique of the pottery and the lamps was clear evidence that the tombs belonged to the EB-MB period. These tombs were differentiated from the Dagger Tombs not only by the grave goods but by the form of the tombs and the burial method. The shafts were deep, up to about four metres (6), and the chambers averaged about 2.50 m. by 2.50 m., though only about 1.40 m. high. The burials again were mostly single, but the skeletons were generally nearly completely disarticulated, having been put into the tombs almost literally as a bag of bones (7).

In the third group the shaft and chamber were even larger; the shaft was up to 5.80 m. deep (one was 7 m.) and the chambers about 3.50 m. by 4.50 m. Another difference was the shaft which was rectangular in plan and not round. The main grave goods consisted of pottery, but with a quite different repertoire of forms than in the Pottery Tombs. The skeletons, once more, were usually disarticulated. This group was given the name Outsize.

These three groups, with four other classes, equally distinct but not so numerous, provide evidence of a population made up of a number of tribal groups, living side by side but following their own separate burial practices. One can probably go further than that and say that some at least of the groups must be semi-nomadic, returning to a tribal headquarters at Jericho at intervals, bringing with them the disarticulated skeletons of those members of the group who had died during the seasonal migration.

A considerable number of such tribal headquarters can be identified in Palestine, the evidence for which is numerous cemeteries but almost no built-up town. The distribution of

6, 7 *Left, above*, the shaft of a Pottery Tomb at Jericho with its entrance intact. *Left, below*, the burial in a Pottery Tomb

8 Plan of a shaft tomb at Megiddo

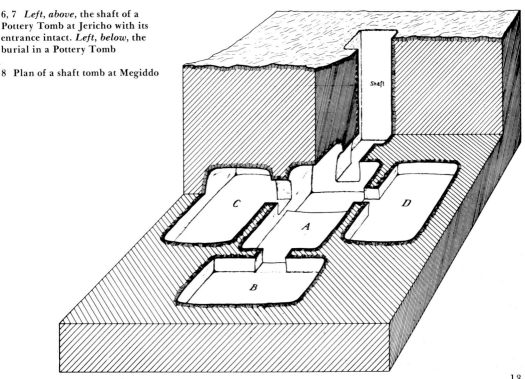

the sites of such cemeteries is shown on fig. 13. There is a family resemblance in the burial practices and particularly in the pottery, but rarely any complete identity. The pottery has in fact been classified into 'families', and this is perhaps the best line of approach. It is not necessary here to describe the characteristics in detail, since all that is relevant here is to stress the tribal, semi-nomadic, non-urban character of those responsible for this interruption of civilised life in Palestine. There can be little doubt that this is the evidence in Palestine of the arrival of the Amurru which the Mesopotamian records document. The nature of the evidence is in itself a reminder that there could be wide local variations present.

To provide the link between Palestine and Syria, reference must be made to the site of Megiddo. There, some buildings within the city may be attributed to the newcomers, though the evidence is not completely sound. Again, there were certainly two, and perhaps

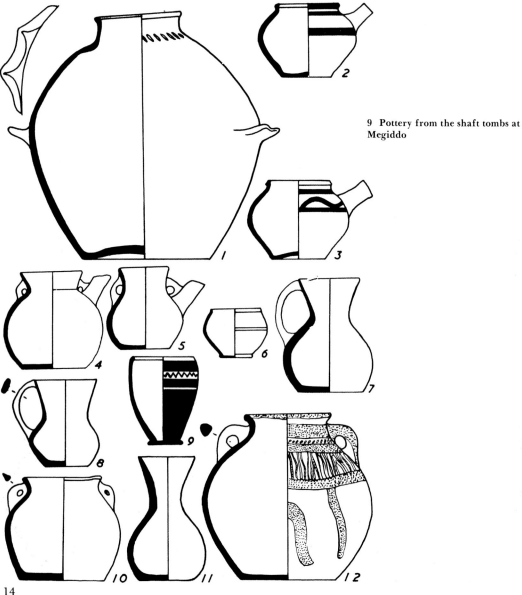

9 Pottery from the shaft tombs at Megiddo

more, classes of burial practice. From the point of view of links with Syria, the most interesting group was that of the shaft tombs. These had a rather elaborate plan (8), with the shaft giving access to a group of chambers. The pottery has enough links with the Outsize tombs of Jericho and with those at Beth-shan to make it certain that they belong to the same general period. With these vessels characteristic of some of the Palestinian groups are others not found elsewhere in Palestine, but well-documented in Syria. Some of these are certainly imports, and the characteristic 'teapot' includes both imports and local copies. These can be compared with vessels from Tell 'As (10). Similar vessels were found at the great site of Qatna, near Homs. Another important find was a group of pins (12), which can be exactly paralleled as a group at Tell Brak, and examples, especially of the club-headed pin (11), provide links with a number of other Syrian sites.

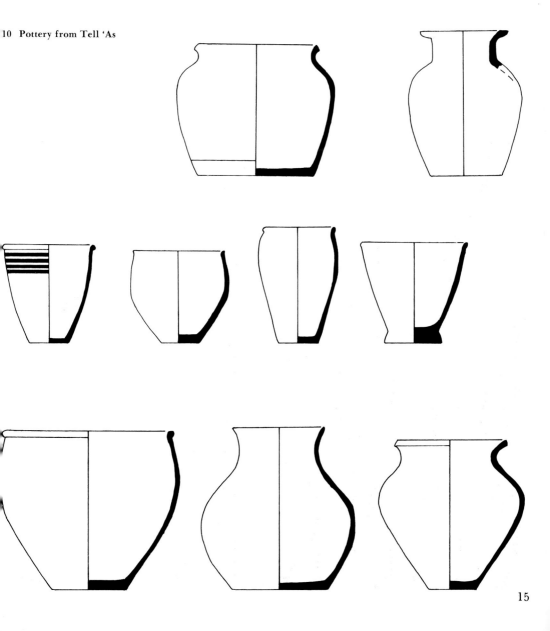

10 Pottery from Tell 'As

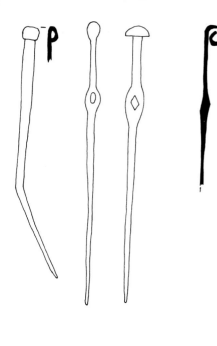

11 Bronze pins from Tell 'As

12 Pins from the shaft tombs at Megiddo

The list of these sites is impressive and they cover a wide area (see map, fig. 13). They stretch from Tell Brak, between the Tigris and the Euphrates on the east, to Byblos and Ras Shamra on the Mediterranean coast, with in-between sites in inland Syria such as Khan Sheikhoun and Tell 'As. At all of these places, as in Palestine, there was a break in urban life.

Ras Shamra was one of the great towns of the coastal area. An impressive mound was built up by occupation beginning in the Neolithic period, with evidence of full urban development in the Early Bronze Age. Into this mound, and beneath the even more impressive town of the Middle Bronze Age, were dug tombs in which the offerings included the club-headed pins. The metal objects, especially the neck torcs, were so striking that the excavator, Professor C. F. A. Schaeffer, called the people concerned the *Porteurs de Torques*. It is possible that at Ras Shamra again there were separate groups, for only one of the tombs published had any pottery (14); this cup has a wavy decoration found on many EB-MB vessels in Palestine.

At Byblos the excavator, M. M. Dunand, recognised the arrival of newcomers, whom he identified as Amorites, at the end of the third millennium. Here, too, there was striking evidence of metallurgy, and it is very possible that among the nomadic or semi-nomadic groups which caused all this disturbance there were groups of itinerant tinkers. Byblos, however, may be an example of a place where there was some urban continuity, and it may have been a centre for the revival of civilisation that marks the beginning of the Middle Bronze Age.

The combined evidence of a break in urban development spreading all over Syria and Palestine, and affecting the major powers in Mesopotamia and Egypt, together with that from tombs of loosely connected groups which were nomadic or only tenuously attached to settled life, shows the very great importance of the nomadic peoples in Western Asia at this time. It is a picture that fits very well the Biblical evidence concerning the Patriarchs. The chronological span of this stage varies in different areas, due no doubt to the degree of civilising influence the preceding civilisations had upon the intruders. At Byblos there is a

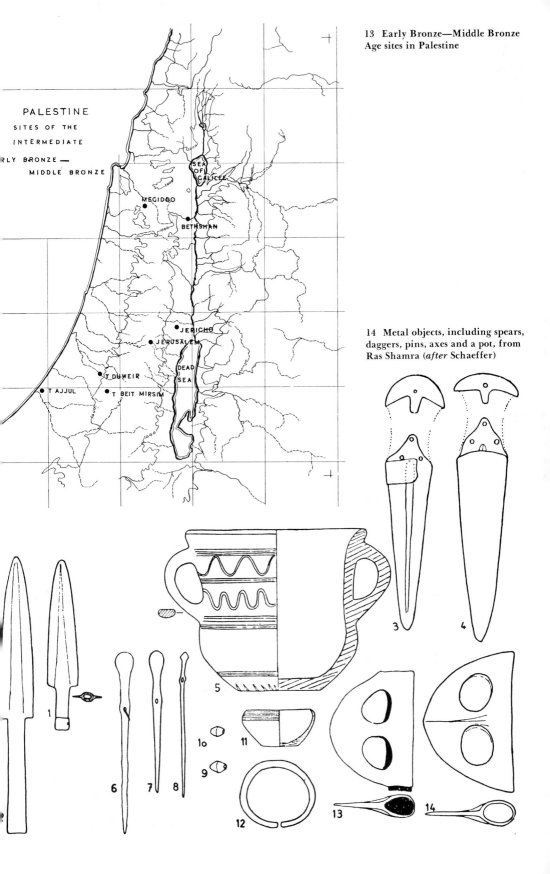

13 Early Bronze—Middle Bronze Age sites in Palestine

PALESTINE

SITES OF THE

INTERMEDIATE

RLY BRONZE —

MIDDLE BRONZE

MEGIDDO

BETHSHAN

SEA OF GALILEE

JERICHO

JERUSALEM

DEAD SEA

T DUWEIR

T AJJUL

T BEIT MIRSIM

14 Metal objects, including spears, daggers, pins, axes and a pot, from Ras Shamra (*after* Schaeffer)

15 Zimri-Lim's palace at Mari. The great court, E, is presumably the place in which groups wishing to appear before the king assembled. To its west, another large court, M, was the centre of the administration, for round it were grouped carefully classified archive rooms. It was dignified by a wall-painting of a king of Mari. The royal quarters could be to the north of this administrative complex, in the north-west quarter of this imposing citadel (*after* Parrot)

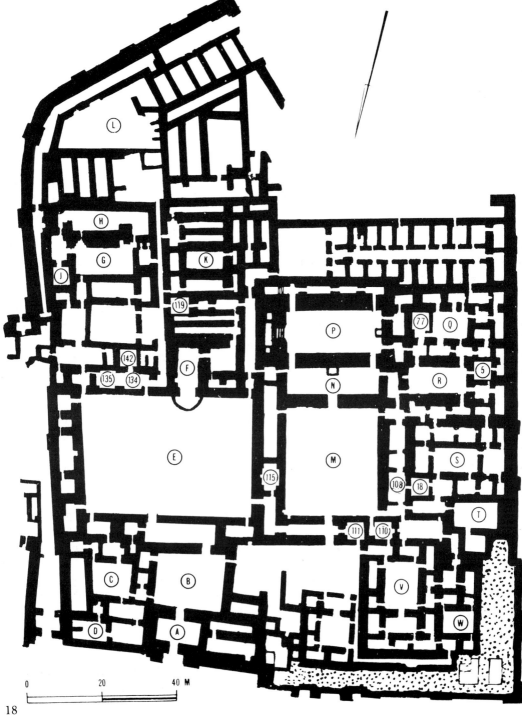

0   20   40 M

gap from about 2185 BC to early in the twentieth century BC, during which period contacts with Egypt were broken. At Ras Shamra-Ugarit a temple had been built on a platform levelled on the summit of the mound in time to receive gifts from Senusret I (1971-1928 BC). In the less civilised area of Palestine to the south, the gap may be longer, perhaps c. 2300 BC to 1900 BC, but there is no close dating evidence so far found.

After the major upset of these Amurru incursions into the settled lands, the city states pushed back the nomads towards the desert fringes and re-established the groups of minor kingdoms, many with an early background, which became the political characteristic of the greater part of the second millennium BC. Some nomadic groups, for instance some of the Amurru themselves, became sedentary. During the first half of the second millennium there were very considerable commercial contacts with Egypt in the coastal area; the extent to which there was any political control is uncertain. In the north and east, there were the competing great powers of the Assyria of Shamshi-Adad I and the Babylonia of Hammurabi, with the Hurrians growing in power. At times subjugated by one or other of the great powers, at times spreading their domains at the expense of one another there were the kingdoms, mainly West Semitic in race, of Mari, Iamkhad (or Aleppo), Qatna and lesser kingdoms such as Ugarit and Alalakh. These kingdoms provided the stable urban element around the borders of which flowed the nomadic groups, the Suteans, the Khanaeans and the Yaminites. Another group was the Habiru, a name linked to Hebrew, but experts debate whether the name has any ethnic significance.

If one accepts that the Patriarchal records go back to this period, their life would be in the setting of these Amorite nomads and seminomads, and they would have known of the urban civilisation of the adjacent kingdoms.

As examples of the urban civilisations one may take Mari, on the bend of the Euphrates, and Ras Shamra. The excavations at Mari have revealed a civilisation of amazing sophistication.

The heyday of Mari was under its most powerful king Zimri-Lim, c. 1780-1760 BC, during the disturbed times of the decline of Assyria and the rise of Hammurabi of Babylon in the late nineteenth to mid-eighteenth centuries. His palace (15) had 300 rooms of which some of the walls were decorated in painted stucco. There were private royal quarters, quarters for the reception of guests and administrative quarters. The most interesting find of all was the royal archives, consisting of some 20,000 tablets of which only 3,000 have so far been published. The documents are mainly administrative or economic. The correspondence of Zimri-Lim covered, mainly on commercial subjects, an area stretching from Dilmun (Bahrein) in the Persian Gulf and Elam in the east to the Phoenician coast and Crete in the west, from Cappadocia in the north to Palestine, notably Hazor and Megiddo, in the south. Legal documents provide interesting parallels to the laws and customs known to the Patriarchs, but it must be remembered that the legal system was that of a settled population, so parallels must not be pressed too far. The organisation of the nomadic tribes whose incursions were a frequent source of trouble to Mari is most usefully described. The Mari documents have enormously extended our knowledge of the background from which the Israelites emerged.

The culture of Mari was that of Mesopotamia; that of Ugarit was coastal. It lies outside the limits usually accepted for Canaan, but its culture is closely related to that of the Canaanite towns the length of the Mediterranean coast. After the interruptions caused by the nomadic incursions, the summit of the mound formed by the buildings of the ancient town was levelled to provide sites for two temples, which later became the temples of Baal and Dagon. The tell site was closely built up, and there was a later extension, similar to that found in a number of other sites, for instance Qatna and Hazor (16), forming a lower town. From the very first stage of this revived urban occupation, the close connection between this northern coastal town with Palestinian towns far to the south is firmly indicated by the pottery. The connection becomes even closer as the Middle Bronze Age civilisation develops in both areas. One can therefore accept a continuum of an urban civilisation the length of the Medi-

terranean. There were cities of major importance such as Megiddo and Hazor (16). Both of these were in correspondence with Mari, and both will reappear in the Biblical record. Jericho was a small town, to which the Biblical account of the Entry into Palestine has given an unjustified importance in this period. The chances of excavation and preservation have, however, made it possible to derive from the site domestic details concerning town life in the Middle Bronze Age, and it should here be emphasised that in this whole Mediterranean seaboard, Canaanite, area there is no break between the revival of urban life in the twentieth century BC and the disturbances of the thirteenth to twelfth centuries BC. It is therefore legitimate to use these Jericho examples of *c.* 1600 BC to illustrate domestic life in the towns into which the Israelites infiltrated.

Very little of Middle Bronze Age Jericho survived subsequent erosion (17), but a small area on the eastern side escaped this erosion. It was clear that the final Middle Bronze Age town was destroyed by a violent fire. Though the burnt remains suffered considerable erosion, enough survived to show the plan of

16 Air view of Hazor with, in the foreground the ancient tell and, to the north, the plateau enclosed in the Middle Bronze Age

17 The tell of ancient Jericho; beyond lies the modern oasis and the mountains of Transjordan

the area (18), and the type of buildings (19). Nothing in the evidence suggests anything grand. Rather narrow cobbled streets climb up the mound from the spring at its eastern foot, and they are flanked by little houses of which the ground-floor, single-room in plan, probably consisted of shops as in many present-day towns in the area, above which were upper storeys with living quarters. This is all very humble, but the evidence supplements the grandiose layouts of Mari and Ras Shamra.

The unique contribution of the Jericho evidence comes from the contemporary tombs. These were quite unlike those of the preceding EB-MB period. They had rock-cut shafts and chambers and were very clearly family vaults. As each member of the family was buried, the earlier bodies and the accompanying grave goods were pushed to the rear of the chamber to create a jumbled mound of bones and offerings. However, when the Middle Bronze Age town of Jericho came to an abrupt end, the final burials of the period were not disturbed, since the families had no successors and therefore the bodies and the accompanying offerings were intact (21). Therefore, from these final tombs full evidence could be obtained of the

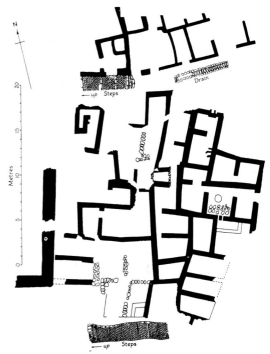

18 Plan of Middle Bronze Age houses at Jericho

19 Houses of MBA Jericho with a street and drain on the left. Top right, layers of burning with a Late Bronze Age wall above them

20, 21 *Above*, reconstruction of a room with MBA furniture based on findings such as those from the tomb, *below*; on the right are the remains of a bed, and to the left a table with a wooden platter

burial practices. It was clear that the dead were buried with the furniture and possessions which they had required during life, and on this basis a reconstruction (20) can be made of the furniture from one of the houses.

It must again be emphasised that this is an illustration of life in a town, albeit a rather humble town. But the period of this final Middle Bronze Age Jericho, early in the sixteenth century BC, is that in which the movements of at least some of the Patriarchs are to be set. This was the sort of life with which the semi-nomads on the fringes between the desert and the fully-cultivated area were acquainted. As they gradually infiltrated into the settled area, they merged into this environment.

As already stated, there was no break in Canaanite culture between the Middle Bronze Age of the first half of the second millennium and the Late Bronze Age of the second half. The political scene changed, with a great spread of Egyptian control resulting from the far-

reaching campaigns of the Pharaohs of the Eighteenth Dynasty and their conflicts with the kingdoms of Mitanni and the Hittites to the north. Among the lesser powers there were changes and fluctuations, but the effects were political rather than cultural. Ugarit can be taken as a good example. Urban life was very flourishing and new quarters were laid out on a regular and orderly plan (22). Many of the houses incorporated stone built tombs, but the method of burial and the type of offerings were very similar to Jericho of c. 1600 BC. To the sixteenth century BC belongs the construction of a magnificent palace which was situated at the western end of the enlarged town (23). The palace covered an area of 10,000 sq. m., and had all the magnificence of the earlier palace of Mari. Like Mari, it had its archives, with different classes of filed documents stored in different places, domestic affairs in one archive, foreign relations with areas to the south in another and documents dealing with the north in a third.

These palace archives are the most recent of the documentary finds from Ugarit. The literary wealth of the site was first revealed by the find of the library associated with the temples of Baal and Dagon which were situated on the mound marking the older town (22). The tablets in this library date from the fifteenth-fourteenth century BC, and are of enormous importance, in the first place on epigraphic grounds, for they are written in an alphabetic script of twenty-nine cuneiform signs. This Ugaritic script played an important part in the development of writing, subsequently perfected by the Phoenicians. The documents in this library covered many subjects, but amongst them are literary texts dealing with the religious myths of the Canaanite pantheon. This Canaanite religion, basically a fertility cult, was the religion of the settled population with which the nomadic Israelites came in touch as they entered the promised land. Palestine itself provides no literary evidence but much material evidence, to which we shall turn in the next chapter.

This then was the the background to the tales of the Patriarchs in the Book of Genesis. It remains here to refer briefly to the question of the historical basis of these tales. The great interval in time before they were put in writing makes it certain that they do not constitute an historical record. Textual and literary critics have discussed in enormous detail how they are to be interpreted. It is generally agreed that the tenth-century editor tried to combine into one story the various accounts that were current

RAS SHAMRA

22 Contour plan of the town of Ras Shamra in which the MBA temples were built on top of the earlier settlement mound. In the Middle Bronze Age the walls of the town enclosed a much larger area with the palace at the western extremity (*after* Schaeffer)

23 **Plan of the palace at Ras Shamra** (*after* Schaeffer)

24 **Plan of houses in the lower town at Ras Shamra** (*after* Schaeffer)

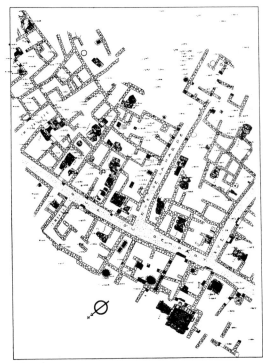

amongst the tribes and groups which had by then become combined into the people Israel. Many authorities agree that there were independent cycles, probably of Abraham-Isaac on the one hand and of Jacob on the other, and that it is only in the redaction that they are given a family relationship. The Abraham cycle probably had its origin in Upper Mesopotamia, the Jacob cycle in Transjordan. Some elements in the story may have an historical basis, some not, but there is almost complete disagreement among authorities as to which can be considered as historical. It is clear throughout that the patriarchal groups were not native to Palestine, but some of the traditions, such as those concerning Shechem, Bethel and Beersheba may reasonably be interpreted as connected with the entry into Palestine of proto-Israelite groups. There is, however, a high degree of probability that there is no connection between the Patriarchal story and the Exodus. The break between the end of the Book of Genesis and the beginning of the Book of Exodus is complete. As to the question of the date of the Patriarchs, authors from Archbishop Ussher (who suggested 4004 BC for the Creation, and the birth of Abraham in 1996 BC, etc.) onwards have selected dates to fit their views. Attempts to provide a chronological link for Abraham with Hammurabi of Babylon as the Amraphel of the four kings against whom Abraham fought need no elaborate discussion to prove that this story has no foundation. The pastoral chief could not be conceived as standing up to the ruler of an imperial power such as Hammurabi. Any attempt to use this as a chronological basis is nonsense.

2 The Entry into Canaan: The Canaanite Background and the Literary Evidence

The religion of the Patriarchs and of Moses was that of worship of a personal, tribal or clan God, the God of my/your/his/father. His name was El, which means simply 'god' in all Semitic languages. This God journeyed with his people, advised them on what to do and promised protection and success. His promise of entry into the land of Canaan is what binds together the stories of Genesis and of the achievement in Exodus-Joshua of the entry and settlement.

This personal religion of the nomads was very different from that of the settled Canaanites. From the Ugaritic tablets we learn that the latter religion was polytheistic, with a pantheon of more than thirty gods. It was an anthropomorphic religion in which the gods exhibited all the human passions and frailties. Although there was this general pantheon, there was not uniformity; states and cities had their own special gods distinguished by individual epithets. El was the original father of the gods, who might be known as El the Warrior or El the Bull. His wife was Asherât. In later texts, El retires into the background, and the leading place is taken by Baal who again has many epithets. His worship and that of his sister and spouse Anat is centred on a purely fertility rite, connected with the dying down and rebirth of vegetation. Around these great gods, or sometimes partially assimilated to them, move others, amongst whom one of the most important is Reshef, god of storms and pestilence.

The Canaanite religion, in varying but allied manifestations, is found the length of the Mediterranean coast as the religion of the settled population (25). Its interest in connection with the Bible is that it is the religion of the towns to which the Israelite groups became neighbours as they moved into Canaan. The evidence of the religion of the cities of Palestine in the fourteenth and thirteenth centuries BC given by the material remains of temples and cult objects is therefore important.

The sites providing the best evidence are Lachish in the south, and Beth-shan and Hazor in the north. At all of these there are structures which from their plans and contents can be identified as temples or sanctuaries. There is thus a basic contrast with the provision made by the non-sedentory Israelite tribes, in which the abode of Yahweh was the tent that sheltered the Ark. It was only Solomon's construction of the Temple in the tenth century BC that gave Yahweh a firmly settled and built home.

At Lachish, excavations revealed a succession of three superimposed temple buildings at the

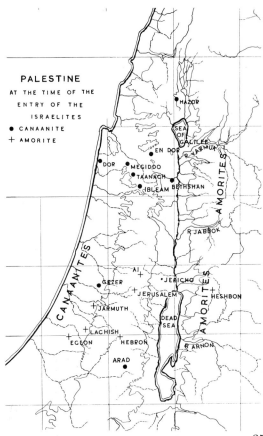

PALESTINE
AT THE TIME OF THE
ENTRY OF THE
ISRAELITES
● CANAANITE
+ AMORITE

25 Palestine at the time of the entry of the Israelites

oot of the mound outside the Middle Bronze Age defences. They range in date from *c.* 1500 BC to late in the thirteenth century. All three successive buildings have a main hall as the central feature, with an altar at one narrow end; the subsidiary rooms varied in the rebuildings. In the earliest structure, three projections in front of the altar (26) may suggest that a triad was worshipped. The cult appurtenances of the third structure (27) are well preserved, and they place strong emphasis on the bringing of offerings to the deity. The main' hall is lined with benches, too close together for use as seats, and therefore intended for the placing of offerings. In the walls were cupboards in which vessels that had contained the offerings were stacked; subsequently they and more mostly offerings of which there was a rich profusion were buried in pits outside the buildings, for they could not return to profane use. Beside the altar were a libation stand for liquid offerings and a bin for solid offerings (28). The deity worshipped cannot be certainly identified. An inscription on an ewer in an archaic script might refer to the goddess Elath or Allat, and a figurine of the Canaanite storm-god Reshef was found. What is in any case clear is that the deity or deities were provided with a long-established home, to which rich offerings were brought.

The successive temples at Lachish were small. It might even be concluded that they were situated outside the town walls since within the town there was official worship of Egyptian gods, for during this period in southern Palestine there was a considerable degree of Egyptian control. At Beth-shan in the north (29), the temples of the time were much more imposing. The summit of the great mound was occupied by religious structures from at least the fifteenth century BC (there may have been earlier ones, but this was the limit of the excavations), down to the time of a Byzantine church. The great interest of the Beth-shan temples is that we have a sequence of structures dating from *c.* 1350 BC (on the current reassessment of the dates) down to the time of the struggles of the Israelites with the Philistines, in which the bodies of Saul and his sons were exposed on the walls of Beth-shan and Saul's armour was placed in the temple of Ashtoreth (I Samuel 31:10). The latest temple of this

26 The foundations of Temple I at Lachish

27 View of Temple III at Lachish

28 Large pottery bin in which solid offerings could be placed in the Lachish Temple

series may have lasted into the time of the Hebrew Monarchy.

The Beth-shan temples vary in plan, but the main element was an assembly hall with a raised altar room at one end. The most revealing element is the cult objects, of which the most striking are the shrine houses and the libation funnels. Snakes and doves form a frequent part of the decoration and can be recognised as symbols of an earth deity (30). Figurines are evidence of the worship of a number of different gods and goddesses, including some with Egyptian connections (31). The emphasis is very clearly on a fertility cult, in which Baal in some form may be presumed to play the most important part.

The great site of Hazor north of Lake Huleh in the Jordan valley, has shown the number of temples that a major town might have. Six belonging to the Late Bronze Age, in use until the thirteenth century, have been identified in the area of the Lower City, of which only part has been excavated, and there may well have been others. The plans have few common features, and there is not enough evidence to decide whether a particular plan was associated with a particular cult. Two of these temples are especially interesting. One was a relatively small and simple structure, built against the back of the earth bank that enclosed the Lower City. In a niche in one long

29 The tell of Beth-shan rising above the valley

30 Pottery cult vessels from the temples at Beth-shan (*after* Rowe)

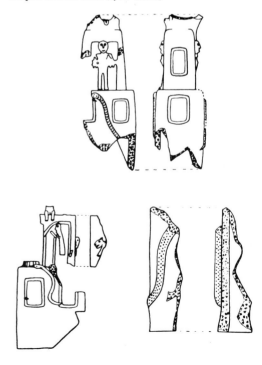

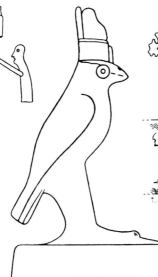

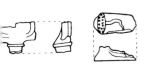

31 Figurines from the Beth-shan temples, some of which show the influence of Egyptian gods, e.g. Hathor and Horus (*after* Rowe)

32 View of the shrine in Area C at Hazor with stelae and a seated figure

wall of the single oblong chamber were set a statue and a row of stelae (32). The statue had on its breast an inverted crescent, and can with some certainty be identified as the moon-god Sin; it is suggested that the central stele, upon which there are carved two arms upraised towards the symbol of the full moon within a crescent moon, represents the consort of the moon-god.

A more important temple was at the extreme north end of the Lower City. The final version, destroyed in the thirteenth century BC was very substantially built in a tripartite plan (33). In the inner room, the largest of the three and clearly the Holy of Holies, was a group of cult objects, altars, libation tables, and large-scale containers or craters. An orthostat carving of a lion, probably set at the entrance into the temple, suggests connections with north Syria or even Anatolia. Fragments of a stone figure showed that the temple had been dedicated to the weather/sun-god, usually known as Hadad or elsewhere as Reshef.

Other towns, too, such as Shechem and Megiddo had their temples, but the examples given are enough to illustrate the flourishing aspects of religion to be found in the Canaanite towns. Moreover, the temples belonged to fully urbanised communities.

This then is the aspect of the country into which the Israelites penetrated. Though, as will be seen, it was long before they capture the great Canaanite cities, their aspect was we known to them and their religion was clearl seductive. Nevertheless, in early stages, it wa felt to be quite appropriate that the nomadi tribes should recognise the local influence of the local gods and should show reverence t them by sacrifices, without impugning th importance of their own god.

We must now turn to a second problem. Th interpretation of the descent into Egypt, th length of the sojourn there and the date an route of the Exodus has, as with so man problems concerning the Pentateuch, produce almost as many theories as there have bee writers. Many of them can appear convincing The one thing that is certainly out of th question (though quite reputable author discuss it at length) is the chronology given i the Bible. It is conflicting within itself. A period of 400 years for the sojourn and th statement that the fourth generation from th descent into Egypt took part in the Exodus are so obviously incompatible that one must dis regard the consecutive account as non historical, and attempt to make the best us one can of the evidence provided in the Biblica record.

33 View of the tripartite temple in Area H at Hazor

Nothing in the Biblical record makes it possible to establish a firm link with extra-biblical history. In fact, various hints or possible inferences can be used to suggest very differing chronologies. The most recent study is that of Father Roland de Vaux, which for the most part I find convincing. He emphasizes the different literary sources detected by many authorities and dissects them convincingly, as well as identifying the characteristics derived from the time of compilation, eleventh-tenth centuries BC, which are anachronistic in relation to the claimed period of the events. The essential feature in this redaction element is that it belongs to a period when the people of Israel in occupation of the whole land of Palestine had become a fact. This conception is carried back into the past, and all the recorded events are considered to be part of the history of the *whole* people of Israel. In fact, as has been already referred to in connection with the Abraham cycle and the Jacob cycle of the patriarchs, many strands are involved, right down to the period of the Judges.

Many writers have sought to see the background of the descent into Egypt, and the influential position acquired by Joseph, in the period of the Hyksos in the seventeenth to sixteenth centuries, in which the Asiatics were dominant in the northern part of Egypt. It would be very difficult to combine this with the most probable date of the Exodus, in the period of Ramesses II, the thirteenth century. In fact, descents of nomadic Asiatics into Egypt were a commonplace, as the Egyptian records, including the famous Beni Hassan paintings, show. The descents were for purposes of trade, in time of seasonal pressure, or even perfectly normal seasonal routine of nomadic groups of which the annual range could cover 500 or so miles. Memories of a descent into Egypt could form part of the tribal (or probably more exactly, clan) oral record of a number of groups of the proto-Israelites. Many Asiatics reached Egypt as prisoners of war, as is clear from the campaign records of the Eighteenth and Nineteenth Dynasty Pharaohs. Asiatic slaves in Egypt from this or other reasons were thus also a commonplace, perhaps forming at least part of the corvée to build the city of Pi-Ramses associated with the Moses story.

It is very reasonable, therefore, to accept that there were many descents. There is also good ground for believing that some groups of proto-Israelites had no tradition of a descent into Egypt. This is probably so with those who became the Transjordan tribes and also those who settled in the north of Palestine. It is probably in this light that one should accept some connection between the 'Apiru-Ḫabiru who troubled western Asia from the time of Mari to that of the Amarna letters in the fourteenth century BC. There is no general acceptance of what, if any, connection there is between the Hebrews and the Ḫabiru, but the most probable solution is that the Hebrews formed a part of a much wider group, the Ḫabiru. When the proto-Israelites entered Palestine, they found settled there elements of the tiresome Ḫabiru of the fourteenth century, with whom ethnic and cultural relationship was acknowledged, and the result was that these earlier settlers were easily integrated. The defeat of Simeon and Levi at Shechem may form part of a tradition of an early, unsuccessful, attempt at settlement.

The incorporation of all the different traditions, from the Patriarchal onwards, is based on the overwhelming importance of the revelations of Yahweh to Moses as described in the Book of Exodus and of the protection by Yahweh of his people in the events of the Exodus. This had to be shown to be part of the history of all the groups that were converted to Yahwehism.

The account of the Exodus in itself is composite. One element is that of a flight, which could be looked upon by the Egyptians as a tiresome disappearance of a useful source of forced labour. The other element is an expulsion, of rebellious slaves or of infiltrating foreigners. There could thus have been the accounts of at least two exoduses combined in the account. Only for one can a reasonable historical background be suggested, the reign of Ramesses II (1304-1237), which is the first period after that of the Hyksos at which the royal residence was in the Delta, the one firm geographical context that we are given. The corvée for the construction of royal and official buildings fits in well as part of the activities of the famous Pharaoh Ramesses II. Historically, one must accept at least one Exodus during his long reign.

When the description of the route of the Exodus is considered Father de Vaux's arguments that two separate routes are combined is very convincing. One traversed the fringe of the south-east corner of the Mediterranean and thence penetrated into southern Palestine; from this were constituted the southern, Judah, tribes. The second, led by Moses, possibly a historical figure, veered far more to the south, into the extremities of the Sinai peninsula (where most of the competing sites of the Mount of God are situated), before proceeding north through Transjordan and then crossing into Palestine north of the Dead Sea. Another possible site for the Mount of God is east of the Gulf of Aqaba, which would have taken them even further afield. A perfectly reasonable interpretation is that this group returned to a pastoral, nomadic, way of life, and proceeded in a leisurely way through these areas in which they could pasture their flocks. This interpretation does, obviously, imply that such a way of life was not so very distant in their past history.

At this stage one can come back to archaeology. So far in this discussion of the descent, sojourn (for the length of which there is no real evidence) and the Exodus, one must be completely dependent on literary and textual criticism, with some reference to the general evidence of history.

3 The Entry into Canaan: The Archaeological Evidence

The theory of two separate entries into Palestine, from the south and from the east, is supported by most modern scholars. They visualise a southern group, entering from the south by the first of the routes just described, and a northern group, in which an entry from the east and the north-east is the essential element.

For the entry from the south, there is no firm archaeological evidence. At the end of the thirteenth century BC, sites in Palestine provide full evidence of destructions (34). But it was a period in which there were areas of widespread destruction, stretching from Anatolia to Egypt. The famous agents in the destruction in which so many great powers succumbed were the Peoples of the Sea, for whom the Egyptian records provide a date of c. 1190 BC. There is archaeological evidence for destruction at a number of sites in southern Palestine from round about 1200 BC, but there is no evidence at all to decide whether these destructions were the work of the Peoples of the Sea, the infiltrating Israelites or even Egyptian campaigns against the Peoples of the Sea. The evidence concerning this entry from the south is textual, though it makes archaeological sense that the infiltration was halted by the line of Canaanite cities of Jerusalem-Ajlun-Gezer.

It is really concerning the entry from the east that most of the modern literary controversy has raged. All sorts of solutions have been proposed for the 'route of the Exodus'. The only dictum that seems to make sense is that of Father de Vaux, that there *was* no route and that it is futile to try and trace it. Over a period of time sufficiently long for almost all of those who left Egypt to have died, the group journeyed gradually north in a perfectly normal nomadic way of life. Forty years in the wilderness is the Biblical expression, but archaeological, physical and anthropological evidence suggests that it was rare in this period of the second millen-

nium for anyone to reach the age of fifty and the real period need only have been twenty to thirty years.

Archaeology has sought to find evidence concerning the period of this Exodus route and entry from the east from what can be learnt concerning the sites in Edom, Moab and Ammon. A most remarkable and very widespread survey by Nelson Glueck suggested that there was a complete lack of sedentary occupation in this area for the greater part of the second millennium. The all-enveloping picture has been altered by the Middle and Late Bronze Age finds in the neighbourhood of the present city of Amman. The general picture has been emphasised by Mrs Bennett's excavations at Umm el Biyara, Tawilan and, especially, Buseira, almost certainly the Edomite capital. There is no firm evidence of urban occupation until about the ninth century BC and an even later date may eventually emerge.

The Exodus group under Moses was therefore not diverted by urban-based kingdoms; but they could equally well have been blocked by a strong tribal-nomadic group. The archaeological evidence for towns in Transjordan is therefore irrelevant.

In the account of the actual entry from the east and of Joshua's campaigns, three sites might be expected to yield evidence and help to establish a chronology; Jericho, 'Ai and Hazor. All have been extensively excavated.

A sounding was made in the mound of Jericho in 1867; it was excavated by an Austro-German expedition from 1907 to 1909, by a British expedition under Professor John Garstang from 1930 to 1936 and by a British expedition from 1952 to 1958 with American and Canadian collaborators in several of the seasons. In the 1930 to 1936 excavations it was claimed that evidence had been found of a destruction of the city in c. 1400 BC, a date which, it was believed, accorded with a dating

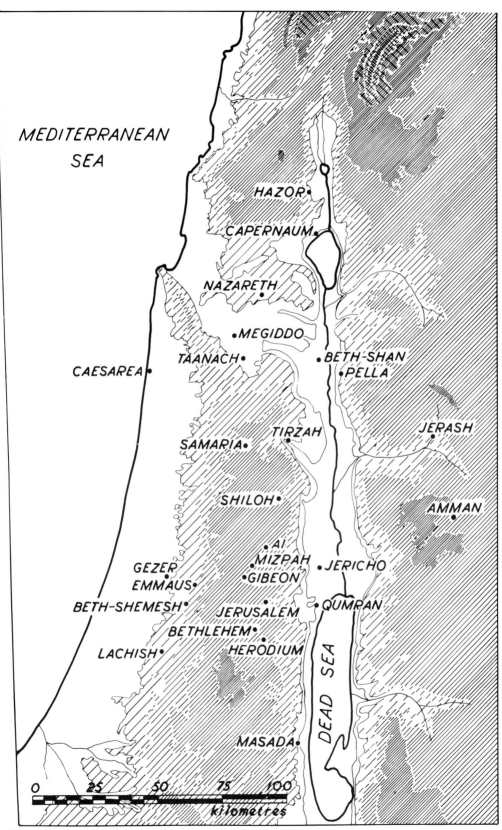

MEDITERRANEAN
SEA

HAZOR •

CAPERNAUM •

NAZARETH •

• MEGIDDO

TAANACH • • BETH-SHAN
• PELLA

CAESAREA •

TIRZAH •

SAMARIA • • JERASH

SHILOH •

• AMMAN

• AI
MIZPAH •
GEZER • • JERICHO
EMMAUS • • GIBEON

BETH-SHEMESH •
JERUSALEM • • QUMRAN
BETHLEHEM •
LACHISH • HERODIUM •

DEAD SEA

• MASADA

```
0        25        50        75        100
```
kilometres

34

method working back from the building of Solomon's temple and adding up the intervening figures for the life of Joshua and the rule of successive Judges—a method of very dubious validity. This claim for the discovery of the walls of the period of Joshua was generally accepted, and appears in many text-books. It is, however, quite wrong.

The description of the capture of Jericho is given in the Book of Joshua. After the death of Moses, following his distant view of the Holy Land from Mount Nebo, the leadership was taken over by Joshua. It is part of the later editor's unification of the entry into the Promised Land that this Moses-led group has, in the account, become the ancestors of all the tribes of Israel, all entering by the route across the Jordan from the east and all taking part in the capture of Jericho as the first event in the conquest. Of the site of Gilgal, where a shrine

was set up to commemorate the crossing of the river, archaeology has completely failed to find any trace.

By the late second millennium BC, there was beside the spring of Ain es Sultan a mound (35) rising some fifty feet above the surrounding plain, built up by the accumulation of collapsed mud-bricks derived from the successive towns on the site over a period from c. 9000 BC. It is generally accepted that this was the site of the town that barred the route into Palestine of the group led by Joshua, though it has to be admitted that there is no absolute proof.

34 Palestine showing principal ancient sites

35 The mound of Jericho from the south. The original land surface was that at the base of the telephone post, and the highest surviving levels belong to around 2300 BC

The story of the capture of Jericho is dramatically told in Joshua 6. After the Israelites, carrying with them the Ark, had marched once round the city on six successive days, on the seventh day they made seven circuits. At the end of this, the trumpets blew mightily and the people shouted and the walls fell down. It has been suggested that a quite reasonable natural explanation is that while the Israelites were investing the town there was an earthquake, which the Israelites very naturally interpreted as Yahweh's intervention on their behalf. Earthquakes are frequent in the Jordan valley, with as many as four major ones a century. The 1952-8 excavations showed that there were no less than seventeen buildings and rebuildings of the city wall during the eight hundred years or so of the Early Bronze Age. Some of the collapses were certainly due to earthquakes. Such evidence can be seen in the line of bricks from the face of a wall which has collapsed from the stones of its foundations to lie face down on the contemporary surface (38). Above is the higgledy-piggledy tumble of the bricks from the core of the wall, and upon this was founded the town wall of the next stage. This could well represent the sort of collapse that enabled the attackers to swarm into the town, but it in fact belongs to a town some one thousand years earlier.

Professor Garstang in his 1930-6 excavations uncovered the remains of a stage in the town wall that had collapsed in this manner, with against it the evidence of a terrific conflagration. This certainly fits the description of the fate of Jericho given in Joshua 6, and it was ascribed by Professor Garstang to this period. Unfortunately, he was misled into believing that this wall belonged to the last stages in the history of Jericho by the chance that erosion had removed much of the evidence. The wall in question in fact belonged to the Early Bronze Age, c. 2300 BC. This wall was the final wall of the Early Bronze Age town. It was succeeded by a camping settlement and then an unwalled village of the EB-MB period that represents the incursion of the semi-nomadic Amorites (p. 10). A walled town was re-established in the succeeding Middle Bronze Age, probably c. 1900 BC. The buildings and culture of these Middle Bronze Age people has been described (p. 20) as an example of the urban civilisations which fringed the semi-desert area in which the wandering of the Patriarchs took place. The Middle Bronze Age town was once more walled. At first these were free-standing walls of mud-bricks, similar to those of the Early Bronze Age, which survived only in the area adjacent to the spring. In the eighteenth century a new system of fortification was introduced in which

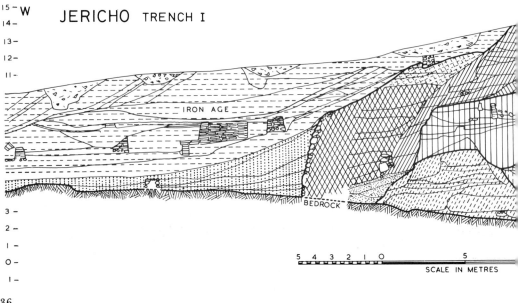

JERICHO TRENCH I

SCALE IN METRES

a great artificial bank was piled up, for the most part on the crest of the pre-existing mound, but on the east side apparently swinging out into the plain. This bank was given a facing of smooth plaster. The height of the defences was thus greatly increased and the angle of approach steepened and given a more slippery surface. The sequence of stages is shown on the sectional drawing of the trench on the west side of the mound (36). Here, the successive walls of the Early Bronze Age town are shown in part. The earlier series is on the right, and is quite clearly succeeded by a later series in the centre; of these, the uppermost, with burnt debris against it, is that ascribed by Professor Garstang to the period of Joshua. The section shows that it was overlain by material of the EB-MB period and buried beneath the massive plaster-faced bank of the Middle Bronze Age, which had two later reconstructions.

However, the complete story is not given in this trench. The western crest of the mound was considerably denuded (37). The complete height of the bank only survives in the north-west corner, where a short stretch of the stone foundations of the wall that originally crowned its summit survives. The whole of the top of the bank and the associated wall has disappeared in erosion over most of the circuit of the town.

37 Vertical air view of the mound of Jericho

36 Jericho, Trench 1. Sloping up against and over the pre-Pottery Neolithic tower are layers of the neolithic periods with successive EB town walls superimposed on them. These are overlain in turn by MB banks

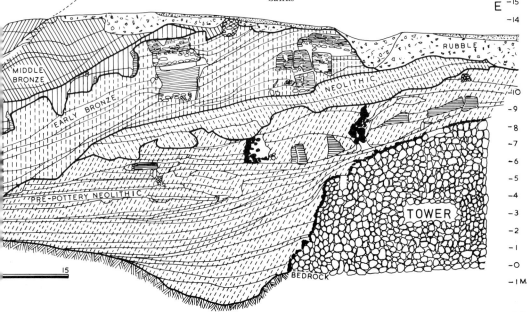

These Middle Bronze Age defences lasted from the eighteenth century to about the middle of the sixteenth century. They could have survived sufficiently to be repaired for use in the Late Bronze Age towns but since so much of the Middle Bronze Age defences have disappeared, it is absolutely certain that nothing at all of walls of the later town, to the period of which the entry into Palestine must belong, can survive. Archaeology will thus never be able to provide visual evidence of the walls that fell down in front of the attacking Israelites.

Excavations have, however, produced enough evidence that there was a Late Bronze Age town and to give some slight evidence of the date at which it was destroyed. Over nearly the whole site the houses of the Middle Bronze Age, and anything later, had shared the fate of the defences and had disappeared due to erosion.

One small area of the Middle Bronze Age town survived on the east side, adjacent to the spring. The houses had been destroyed by fire at the end of the Middle Bronze Age, in the first half of the sixteenth century BC. After, it is certain that there was then an abandonment during which erosion carried the burnt debris down the slope of the mound, to create a thick layer over the seventeenth-sixteenth century houses. Overlying this debris layer there survived at the east end of the excavated area the stone foundations of a single wall. This wall was so close to the modern surface that only about a square metre of the contemporary floor survived, with elsewhere the modern surface cutting down into it (40). The one juglet surviving on its surface, lying by a small clay oven, and a limited amount of Late Bronze Age pottery beneath the floor, suggests that the

38 Example of a town wall of the Early Bronze Age destroyed by earthquake. At the base, beside the survey pole, the stone foundations and, spreading to the right, the face of the brick wall collapsed onto the contemporary surface

39 MB houses overlain by burnt debris with, above them, the foundations of the wall seen in fig. 40

building is late fourteenth century in date. A Late Bronze Age occupation of the site is thus proved, but the excavations within the town provide little detail.

The best evidence for dating the re-occupation of the site after a period of abandonment at the end of the Middle Bronze Age comes from the tombs excavated during the 1930-36 excavations. Professor Garstang was misled in the interpretation of the evidence from them by then current misdatings of sixteenth to fourteenth century pottery. He also failed to realise that in the process of burial in these rock-cut tombs, the latest burial is usual at a low level in front of the tomb, with the remains of earlier burials pushed back and mounded up to the rear (41). Absolute height of burials within the tomb chamber means nothing, and Professor Garstang was led to

believe that later objects found on the same level as earlier ones were contemporary. A wholly false impression of continuity and early chronology was thus given. The finds in the tombs cleared in these excavations indicated that a very few of the Middle Bronze tombs were re-opened and some later burials were placed in them.

Associated with the burials in this period of Late Bronze Age re-use there were Mycenaean vessels. Unfortunately no sufficiently diagnostic features survive to pin-point the period of these tombs. The acknowledged leading authority on the subject, Professor Furumark, considers that the finds cannot be more closely dated than within the period of LM IIIA (1425 to 1300 with internal divisions) and LM III B (1300-1230 BC). Mrs Hankey, however, would put the vessels concerned in LM III A 2 (1375-

1300). The attribution of the vessels within LM III is not sufficiently precise to provide close dating. The only thing that is important is that one can say on the basis of archaeological evidence that there was a break in continuity at the end of the Late Bronze Age re-occupation. It would be very difficult on the pottery evidence to put this as late as the end of the thirteenth century. The general evidence, both from the Mycenaean pottery and the other wares would allow for a date as late as 1300 BC but not later. After this occupation ceases until Iron Age II.

The evidence from 'Ai is still more disappointing. 'Ai ceased to be a town of any importance at the end of the Early Bronze Age before the end of the third millennium. The most recent excavator, Professor Callaway, ha identified a modest Iron Age village, in which two stages can be recognised. He suggests that the first of these was the one on which the attack in the Book of Joshua is so vividly described. The pottery found does not suggest a date that could belong to an early stage in the entry of the Israelites, and the break between the two stages seems very slight. Many efforts have been made to explain away the 'Ai evidence, but none are really satisfactory. Aetiology must play a part, and de Vaux points out the resemblance to the attack on the

40

Benjaminites at Gibeah, which may have been transferred to 'Ai to salve the pride of the Benjaminites. On the whole, the probability is that there is no historicity in the story of the attack on 'Ai.

Concerning Hazor we are much better informed. The city was destroyed late in the fourteenth century BC, possibly in 1318 BC by Seti I, or possibly as late as 1300 BC. It was immediately rebuilt, mostly without change of plan, but the buildings were of greatly inferior construction. This city was again destroyed after apparently a short interval, and was violently burnt. This would agree with the description in the Book of Joshua. The pottery belonging to this latest Late Bronze Age city is certainly not as late as the end of the thirteenth century BC, for instance as that of Lachish Temple III and Tell Beit Mirsim level C 2. The Mycenaean pottery includes a little very late LM III A 2 or very early LM III B. It therefore extends into the thirteenth century BC, though not necessarily very far into it. Thereafter, Hazor suffered a severe eclipse. The lower city was permanently abandoned, and when the upper city was re-occupied in the Iron Age, it was only an insignificant village. The destruction of Jericho and the destruction of Hazor may be separated by as much as fifty years, but it might be as little as twenty-five.

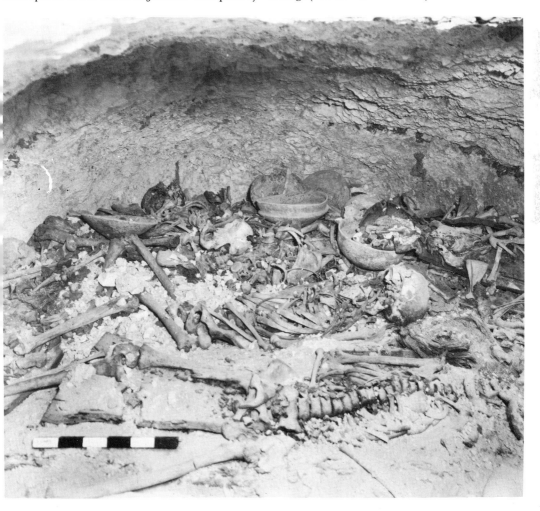

40 LB Jericho: centre, foundations of LB house with, left, a small area of the contemporary floor

41 A Jericho tomb with the latest burial in the foreground, and earlier burials pushed to the back

Literary criticism has proposed at least three main infiltrating groups, originally separated by barriers of strong Canaanite towns; one from the south associated with Judah and an expulsion Exodus; another from the east into the mountains of Ephraim, associated with Benjamin, and a third in the north, where the tribes of Naphthali and Issachar are the principal participants in the Battle of the Waters of Merom against Yabin, king of Hazor. This latter battle de Vaux convincingly separates from the Battle of the Waters of Megiddo, celebrated in the Song of Deborah and generally accepted as of twelfth century date, when Hazor was certainly non-existent. A case can also be made out that most of the proto-Israelites in the north had infiltrated over a long period, possibly including that of the Ḫabiru, and did not have a tradition of a descent into Egypt.

If one accepts this basic division, what the archaeological evidence is saying is that by 1275-1250 BC in the north the proto-Israelite groups concerned had become powerful enough and sufficiently cohesive to defeat the local representatives of settled urban life, Hazor, when that city tried to oppose their expansion from the relatively thinly-populated, heavily wooded area of the northern hill-country. Acceptance of the chronology suggested by the Hazor archaeological evidence, therefore involves no difficulty. I would prefer a date of c. 1275 BC to the later thirteenth century BC suggested by Professor Yadin, but the difference is not serious. In the thirteenth century BC proto-Israelite infiltration had become important.

In the southern area, there are far too many other possibilities to make it possible to say that a destruction indicated by archaeological evidence as belonging to the last third of the thirteenth century BC was the work of the Israelites. Other competitors are the Sea Peoples (from whom the Palestinian Philistines evolved), the Egyptian forays or expeditions to meet these Sea People invasions, and any local process of interacting hostility which could at any stage have emerged. One can only note that c. 1230-1200 BC there were a number of serious destructions on town sites.

The entry into the central area, the Mountains of Ephraim, which is essentially the sto[ry] of the Benjaminites and the House of Josep[h] has as its highlight the leadership of Joshua an[d] the capture of Jericho. There seem to b[e] grounds for believing that Joshua was a histori[cal] cal leader. The story of the capture of Jericho certainly dramatic enough and detailed enoug[h] to make one inclined to accept it. But on[e] cannot fit in an Exodus during the reign [of] Ramesses II, say c. 1250 BC, followed by leisurely progress across Sinai and up the dese[rt] fringes of Transjordan with a crossing of th[e] Jordan and a destruction of Jericho which, o[n] present archaeological evidence, must be som[e] where about the beginning of the thirteent[h] century.

Various efforts have been made to solve th[e] problem. Many scholars, as with 'Ai, invok[e] aetiology. They suggest that one of the trad[i]tions incorporated by the later redactor sough[t] to explain these ruins by ascribing them to th[e] work of Joshua's band; the story of the captur[e] would either have been invented, or, as som[e] suggest, be some sort of ritual, possibly wit[h] some sort of relationship with the sanctuary o[f] Gilgal, which cannot be very far away. Th[e] aetiological explanation has never appealed t[o] me, mainly because I find it difficult to believ[e] that the early Israelites would have recognise[d] this mound as a ruin, the product of huma[n] activity. It would not have taken many decade[s] for rain and wind to have reduced the de[s]troyed mud-brick buildings to the mound o[f] earth one sees today (37), and there would b[e] no need to explain it.

Another explanation suggested, includin[g] recently by de Vaux, is that since excavatio[n] has shown that the town of the fourteenth cen[tury] tury has been almost completely washed away[,] there may have been a later one, of the thir[t]teenth century of which not even the slightes[t] remnant survives. This is theoretically quit[e] possible, but there is clear evidence against it[.] When layers are washed off the top of a[.] mound, they must be washed somewhere[.] Broken mud-brick could to some extent b[e] blown away in a wind, but not heavier object[s] and in particular the all-important potsherds[.] These should be found in the wash at the foo[t] of the slopes. The thirteenth century potsherd[s] simply do not exist anywhere on the site. The learest evidence came from Trench I, where a trip 18 m. long at the foot of the Middle Bronze Age defences was cleared. This is where sherds derived from the hypothetical vanished town should have been found, but they were not.

The conclusion arrived at, then, is that the only way in which the conflicting evidence can be reconciled is by further fragmentation. Two Exoduses have already been suggested. Either there must have been yet another, not connected with events that suggest the time of Ramesses II, or the capture of Jericho belongs to a completely different strand in the subsequent compilation, and yet another group entering Palestine.

Of the early stages of settlement in Palestine and the period of the Judges, archaeology tells us almost nothing. Gradually pottery and other objects characteristic of the Late Bronze Age disappear, but it is extremely difficult to say of any one site that one layer is Canaanite, the next Israelite. The answer is that the penetration of the Israelites was very gradual, much of it peaceful, and everywhere in close contact with the Canaanite villages. The Canaanite towns did not fall into their hands until quite late. Part, therefore, of the settlement was relatively peaceful merging, part was more intensive occupation of the country, mainly in the wooded hill-country to the north, where Professor Aharoni has identified settlements with pottery of the twelfth-eleventh centuries. To this stage belongs the re-occupation of Hazor by people living in a poor, unwalled village on the ancient tell, leaving the great Middle Bronze Age addition unoccupied.

The Judges were local leaders who rallied varying elements of the population in times of danger. The threats of danger came mainly from the Philistines on the coast. These consisted of elements of the People of the Sea pushed back from Egypt by Ramesses III at a date now usually considered to be *c.* 1170 BC. Pottery associated with them can be identified, but little in fact is known of their culture. For Biblical history, their importance is that they forced the people of Israel to amalgamate into a monarchy. Saul was ultimately defeated by them, but his successor David ruled the first united Israel.

4 Palestine in the Time of David and Solomon

At the end of the eleventh century we reach a period at which the contribution both of the literary record and of archaeology becomes very different from that of the preceding period. The historical books of the Bible are a near-contemporary record. They are not written quite from the viewpoint of a modern historian, for the religious element remains all-important; they are still basically a record of Yahweh's dealings with his people. There is also still no firm chronological framework. Lengths of reign, or other periods in calendar years, are very much more reliable than for all figures recorded down to and including the Book of Judges, though confusion can arise from the relation of the period of a reign to the seasonal calendar. Moreover, the Jewish seasonal calendar cannot of itself be related to the modern calendar. For this it is still dependent on the Egyptian calendar. However, the Biblical account and connected historical events are sufficiently numerous and detailed for terms in calendar years to be given to events in Palestine within limits of only a year or so. The first event that can be dated with precision is the death of Solomon in 925 BC.

The contribution of archaeology is also much more precise. By the end of the eleventh century, the Israelite tribes were firmly settled in towns and villages, with a developed material culture of their own. The history of these towns and villages can be traced by archaeological excavation in a way that was impossible in connection with the more primitive remains of the beginnings of the Israelite settlement and still more in connection with the background that lay behind the settlement. Over the last thirty-five years the archaeological evidence from many major sites has become available.

The story begins with the reign of David. Saul had, for a brief period, led a combination of the Israelite tribes against the Philistines, but his leadership ended with the battle of Mount Gilboa. David's emergence as his successor was complicated. He had served as a successful mercenary with the Philistines. His reputation as a warrior was the basis of his appointment by the southern tribes as a leader. The effects of the separate entry-routes of the tribes, described in the last chapter were, in the late eleventh century, still apparent in their groupings and alliances. The progress northward of the tribes entering from the south had been gradual, and its northern limit was circumscribed by the line of Canaanite cities Jerusalem-Ajlun-Gezer.

David shortly afterwards also became king of the northern tribes, being chosen by them for the same reason that had motivated the southern tribes, his military prowess. In effect at this stage he held two separate, elective, kingships. The United Monarchy of Israel that emerged was his personal creation. To construct this unified kingdom he had to join the two areas geographically, and this meant removing the barrier of Canaanite towns between the northern and southern groups. Most essential of all was the capture of Jerusalem. The geography of Palestine is such that regular communications between the north and the south are virtually confined to the coastal plain, over which the Philistines held control, and a narrow strip along the crest of the mountain range. Commanding this strip at its narrowest part was Jerusalem. Though a capture of Jerusalem is claimed in the Book of Joshua, the more realistic account is given in Joshua 15:63 which states, 'As for the Jebusites the inhabitants of Jerusalem, the children of Judah could not drive them out: but the Jebusites dwell with the children of Judah at Jerusalem unto this day'. That this was the case is shown by the fact that one of the first acts of David was the capture of Jerusalem. This not only opened up the route between his southern and northern ingdoms, but also gave him a capital that was is own, outside the jurisdiction of either tribal roup.

Excavations at Jerusalem on a large scale egan in 1867, following the establishment of he Palestine Exploration Fund in 1865. The EF's interests were concentrated on the Old ity of Jerusalem (42), so-called today to dis- nguish it from the new growth to the west hich began in the nineteenth century and has ow reached enormous proportions. The Old ity is in fact relatively modern. The walls that urround it are in origin the work of Suleiman he Magnificent in the sixteenth century AD, nough the plan is derived from that of the

Roman city of the second century AD (see p. 99). Its south-east corner is dominated by the great artificial platform, at present known as the Haram esh-Sherif, on which is situated the magnificent Moslem sanctuary of the Dome of the Rock (43). This platform is the only really ancient feature to survive in the Old City, having been created by Solomon to provide the setting for his Temple, and in its present form representing the much enlarged platform con- structed by Herod the Great in the first century BC for his rebuilding of the Temple.

42 Jerusalem, seen from the east, with the Dome of the Rock on the right

43 Interior of the Old City of
Jerusalem

Though the excavators of the Palestine Excavation Fund, of whom the most distinguished was Captain Charles Warren, RE, gave most of their attention to the site of the Temple and other features within the Old City, it emerged from these investigations and others down to the end of the nineteenth century that remains of ancient Jerusalem were to be found to the south of the Old City. This area is bounded on the east by the Kedron valley, above the north end of which towers the Temple platform, and on the west by the Hinnom valley (the Biblical Gehenna) which curves round from the south-west corner of the Old City to join the Kedron some 625 m. south of the south wall of the Temple platform. Between the two, much filled by debris, and only just visible in the air photograph (44), is a central valley, called by

44 Jerusalem from the air. On the right is the Kedron valley, on the left, the Hinnom valley. To the south of the present Old City is the site of the earliest town. The narrow eastern ridge is divided from the western by a less well-defined valley

Jerusalem in the time of the
[Je]busites and David. Excavations
[ha]ve shown that the east wall of the
[fir]st town was low on the slope of
[th]e Kedron valley and that the
[no]rth wall crosses the eastern ridge
[at] a distance of about 300 m. south
[of] the present Old City. The rest of
[th]e circuit is deduced from existing
[co]ntours

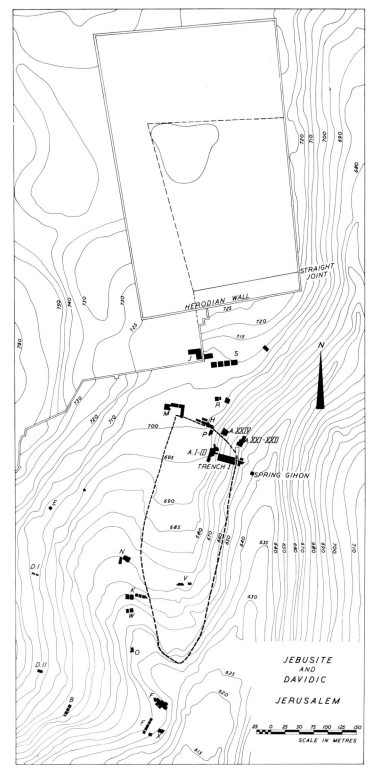

STRAIGHT
JOINT

N

HERODIAN WALL

J   S

R

M   H

P   A. XXIV

A. XXI - XXII

A. I-III

TRENCH I   SPRING GIHON

E

N

D.I

V

K

W

O

D.II   JEBUSITE
AND
DAVIDIC

B   F

JERUSALEM

F
X

25 0 25 50 75 100 125 150

SCALE IN METRES

Josephus the Tyropoeon, which divides the area into an eastern ridge and a western ridge.

The excavations of the late nineteenth century and first half of the twentieth were concentrated in the area to the south of the Old City, for it was recognised that this was where Old Testament Jerusalem was to be found. Nevertheless, when *The Bible and Archaeology* was written in 1940, very little of the structural history of Jerusalem was known, and many conclusions drawn up to that time were wrong.

The excavations carried out between 1961 and 1967 by the British School of Archaeology in Jerusalem on behalf of a large number of institutions of which the most important was the British Academy, and with the collaboration of the École Biblique and the Royal Ontario Museum, have at least put Old Testament Jerusalem on the map with some precision, even though the structural remains are scanty.

The original city of the Jebusites and of the Israelites from the time of David at least to the eighth century BC lay entirely on the eastern ridge (45). The main contribution in respect of the plan of early Jerusalem of the 1961-67 excavations was to show that the line of the east wall was situated not on the crest of the ridge but well down the slope, and that the north wall crossed the ridge some 230 m. south of the walls of the Old City. The position of the city was dictated by the water supply. The only perennial spring was the Spring Gihon, the Virgin's Fountain, in the Kedron valley. This would have been far outside the walls if they had been, as the earlier excavators supposed, on the crest of the ridge. Access to a vital water supply from within a city by a shaft or gallery is a well-established feature of Palestinian town planning. Such a shaft and gallery exists at Jerusalem, but its head lies well outside the wall on the crest. This was the first problem tackled in 1961, with a trench down the slope from the wall on the crest exposed by the 1923-5 excavations in the direction of the spring. The wall on the crest was shown to be Maccabean (Hellenistic) in date, with the earliest stage Post-Exilic, probably of the time of Nehemiah in the fifth century BC. The original wall (46), dating from the eighteenth century BC, repaired by David and continuing in use to the eighth

century BC, was found to be 48 m. further east and well down the slope (47). It was so situated as to give good protection to the rock-cut shaft to the spring, and near enough to the latter to prevent enemy interference with the (presumably) blocked-up entrance to the spring, but not so low in the valley as to bring it within the range of projectiles from the opposite slope.

This eastern wall was excavated only at the one point, but its course to the south, to the well-marked southern point of the ridge, can be inferred with some probability. The course up the slope to the north-west from the section exposed and thence west across the crest was established, though the wall itself was not found. On the west side it must have followed the well-marked rock scarp, though no part of the structure survives.

Nothing of the lay-out of the town within the walls, either of the Jebusite or Israelite period, has been recovered, and it is unlikely that any remains will ever be found. On the eastern slope the Jebusites had constructed a system of terraces, supported by massive stone substructures. These are most imposing, and represent a tremendous building operation, but they were essentially unstable. Any collapse of the outer retaining wall would be followed by the crumbling of the substructure behind. In the area cleared a number of repairs of the substructures was found. This is in fact highly probably the enigmatic *millo* (filling), in the Biblical account repaired by successive rulers from David onwards. The terrace system collapsed in a great cascade of stones after the Babylonian destruction of Jerusalem in the early sixth century. Only a very small area of the seventh century houses at the head of the slope was still intact, and nothing of earlier houses survived earlier collapses. Therefore Jebusite, Davidic, Solomonic and later structures in the part of Jerusalem which was on the eastern slope have disappeared in collapses. It would be very good luck if an area that had escaped these collapses could be found.

The part of Jerusalem on the narrow summit of the ridge was much more stable but, whilst not subject to obliteration by collapses, unfortunately it has disappeared even more completely as the result of another destructive agent, that of quarrying. It is likely that com

The eastern wall of Jerusalem
uld not have been lower down
e slope since it would have been
mmanded by the missiles of
emy forces on the opposite side of
e valley

siderable damage was done to the earliest remains even within the Old Testament period, for cisterns, baths and other rock-cut features, probably of the Hellenistic period, can be identified. The really wholesale destruction by quarrying, however, came in the Roman period when the area of earliest Jerusalem was left outside the walls. Wherever any site on the summit has been excavated by successive expeditions, the evidence can now be certainly interpreted as showing quarrying, with the only intact levels belonging to the Byzantine period. The most dramatic evidence of this quarrying was exposed in the French excavations of 1912-13 (48), where a few fragments of the lower part of the rock-cut cisterns and baths survive, but elsewhere quarrying has gone deep into bedrock. Old Testament Jerusalem was in fact obliterated to build Roman Aelia Capitolina in the time of Hadrian.

Archaeology has not revealed much of the period of David outside Jerusalem. David, in fact, was not a great builder; his time was fully occupied with expanding his domain. Having created a strong base by unifying all the Israelite tribes into a single kingdom, he then brought under his control a wide area, which at

its maximum extended from Damascus in th[e] north to the Gulf of Aqaba in the south (49[). Israel at that time was in power and extent a[s] important as any of the kingdoms of wester[n] Asia. Solomon failed to maintain this great[er] Israel, but it was the basis of the wealth an[d] prestige of his long rule in Jerusalem.

For the period of Solomon the archaeologic[al] finds of the past thirty years have much t[o] contribute. We know from the Biblical accou[nt] something of the magnificence of Solomon['s] Jerusalem. The archaeological contributio[n] has been to emphasise the significance of wha[t] we know of its plan and to enable us to form a[n] idea of its appearance from knowledge of co[n]temporary art and architecture. No actu[al] remains of Solomonic Jerusalem have survive[d].

Solomon's contribution to Jerusalem was th[e] Temple and his adjoining palaces, described i[n] great detail in I Kings 5-7. All this was d[e]stroyed in the Babylonian conquest of Jerus[a]lem in 587 BC. Anything that may have su[r]vived this destruction disappeared beneath th[e] rebuilding of the Temple by Herod the Gre[at] or in the quarrying of stone that accompanie[d] this rebuilding.

Solomon's Temple and palaces had to [b]

utside the Davidic city, for structures on the
ale he had in mind would have required
most the whole built-up area. Expansion to
e north was not difficult, for the eastern ridge
ere runs back towards the main line of hills
ithout any real break. There were, neverthe-
ss, considerable physical difficulties. The
mmit of the ridge was narrow. The provision
any large level area required the construc-
on of an artificial platform supported by
owerful retaining walls. The walls visible to-
ay at the south-east corner of the Herodian
emple platform rest on the steep rock slopes

of the Kedron valley at a depth of some 50 m.
below the ground level of the courtyard inside
them (50). One can now say that, at least at this
point, the substructures of Solomon's temple
courtyard must have been almost equally
massive (51).

It is possible to make this deduction, since
the position of the south-east corner of Solomon's platform can now be identified with a
considerable degree of probability. We know
from the account of the first century AD Jewish
historian Flavius Josephus that Herod the Great
doubled the size of the Temple platform in his

Map showing the conquests of
avid

Quarrying on the summit of the
stern ridge which removed all
ildings of the first millennium

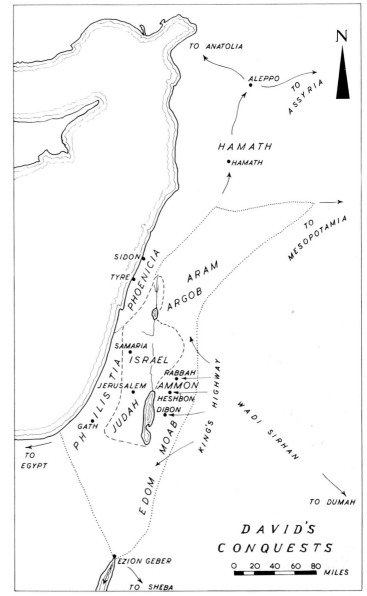

TO ANATOLIA

ALEPPO

TO ASSYRIA

N

HAMATH

•HAMATH

TO MESOPOTAMIA

SIDON•

TYRE•

PHOENICIA

ARAM

ARGOB

SAMARIA

ISRAEL

RABBAH

JERUSALEM AMMON

HESHBON

DIBON

JUDAH

MOAB

KING'S HIGHWAY

WADI SIRHAN

GATH

PH...ILIS

TO
EGYPT

EDOM

TO DUMAH

DAVID'S
CONQUESTS

0 20 40 60 80
━━━━━━━━━━━━ MILES

EZION GEBER

TO SHEBA

great rebuilding of the first century BC. Herod's characteristic masonry is visible in the external south and west faces of the platform. On the east side, it ends abruptly against an earlier structure of entirely different masonry (52). This must belong to the platform of the preceding Temple, that is to say the original Second Temple, which owed its origin to Zerubbabel after the return from the Babylonian exile, and was completed in 515 BC. The style of masonry agrees with this, for it is similar to that of the Persian period at Byblos and Eshmoun, near Sidon. The restoration of Jerusalem by the returned exiles, according to the literary evidence, made much use of surviving fragments of the earlier buildings, as is entirely natural. It is highly probable that considerable portions of the great platform on which Solomon's Temple stood were still visible, and much the easiest way to restore the Temple would have been to re-use the surviving foundations. Almost certainly, therefore, this straight joint gives us the position of the south-east corner of Solomon's Temple platform. No comparable straight joint is visible in the west wall, where Herodian masonry is visible for a distance of 180 m. The earlier west wall must therefore lie inside the Herodian platform. Its

position is probably somewhere near the li[ne] suggested on the plan (53), and the elevation [of] the Solomonic south wall may be that show[n] (51), with the platform confined to the easte[rn] ridge, as was the rest of the early city.

The Solomonic Temple thus lay some 232 [m] to the north of the north wall of the David[ic] city. Its site was joined to this earlier city by [a] narrow strip on the summit of the ridge. Ev[i-]dence for the line of the east wall of th[e] extension has been found, and the line of th[e] west wall can be inferred, though with le[ss] certainty. The extension would have provide[d] the space required by Solomon for his palac[e] and administrative buildings. From the Bib[li-]cal account we know that when he built th[e] Temple, he also built his palace and a palac[e] for his principal wife, the daughter of th[e] Egyptian Pharaoh. It is highly probable tha[t] these palaces were in this area, for there wou[ld] have been little room for them on the Templ[e] platform. Also within this area one can suppo[se] that there were the administrative building[s] required for the officials needed to run th[e] elaborate organisation of the kingdom of whic[h] the Biblical account gives some detail. Un[-]fortunately, no trace at all survives of thes[e] buildings. All the excavations of the 1961-6[

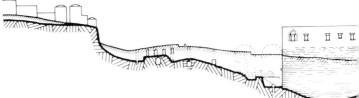

50, 51 *Above*, the south elevation of the Herodian Temple platform. *Below*, a conjectural elevation of the Solomonic Temple platform of which the position of the south-east corner is certain, and the south-west corner is deduced

52 On the right, masonry which probably represents the Zerubbabel rebuilding of the Temple platform against which the Herodian platform is built with a straight joint

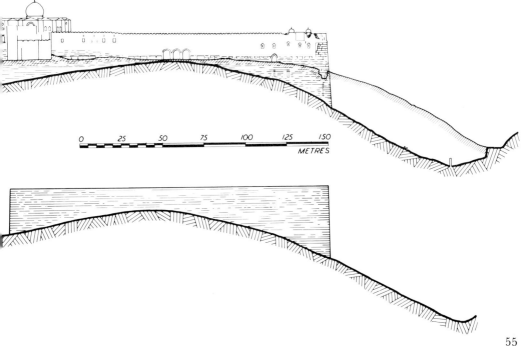

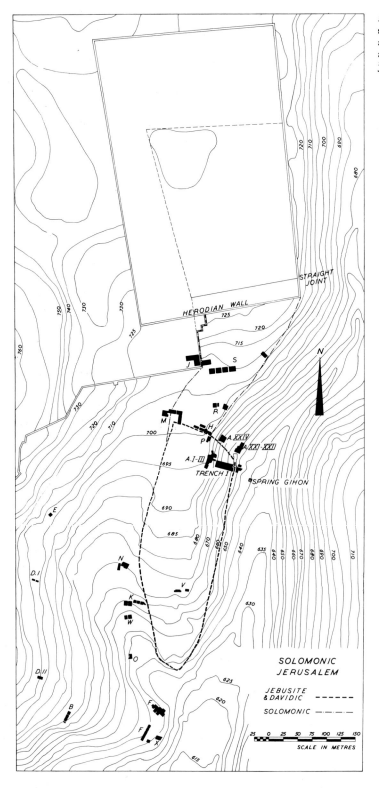

53 Plan of Solomonic Jerusalem showing the extension from the area of the Jebusite-Davidic period and the location of the straight joint seen in fig. 52

SOLOMONIC
JERUSALEM

JEBUSITE
& DAVIDIC   – – – – – –

SOLOMONIC   –·–·–·–

25 0 25 50 75 100 125 150
SCALE IN METRES

expedition, of which the position is shown on the plan (53), produced clear evidence of quarrying at periods from the Herodian down to Byzantine, in which all evidence of earlier structures has disappeared. The more recent excavations under Professor Mazar, in the area between the Herodian platform wall and the Site S trenches, likewise found nothing early.

Archaeology has thus now provided a fairly firm outline plan of Solomon's Jerusalem, but Jerusalem itself has produced almost no structural remains. One has to visualise what the buildings looked like from the Biblical account. Fortunately, archaeological evidence from other sites can now add something to the picture. The Bible gives the key, in that it shows how much Solomon was influenced by contemporary fashions in the adjacent states of western Asia. The contrast between the long history of urban life and advanced material culture in these states as compared with that of the Israelites, so recently nomadic or semi-nomadic tribal groups, has already been emphasised. The most advanced material culture in the tenth century BC was that of coastal Phoenicia. Solomon therefore turned to Hiram King of Tyre for materials and craftsmen (I Kings 5: 5-6). The excellence of Phoenician masonry is well illustrated at Ras Shamra-Ugarit in the late second millennium. That this type of masonry was borrowed by the Israelites in the first millennium is proved by the excavations at Samaria (71), where Omri and Ahab were also under Phoenician influence. One can therefore infer that the Solomonic buildings in Jerusalem were in a similar style.

One can also infer that the decorations of the Temple, vividly described in the Bible, and the other buildings were in Phoenician style. Here again, the ivory carvings found at Samaria provided a clue, but far more has been learnt from Sir Max Mallowan's excavations at Nimrud in Assyria between 1949 and 1962. All these finds were of ivory carvings applied to furniture, for instance to beds (54) and chairs. The decoration of the interior of the Temple was on a much larger scale, and nothing comparable has survived. One can, however, easily visualise the mysterious cherubim guarding the Ark in the Holy of Holies by comparison with carvings from Nimrud (55).

It is also possible to suggest what the plan of Solomon's palace may have been from evidence in Syria. The plan of two palaces at Sendchirli (56) would fit well the description of that of Solomon, with a combination of reception halls, courts and private quarters. The other buildings, administrative, for archives and so on, which it is suggested occupied the new quarter, may also be on the lines of buildings so identified at Ugarit and Mari, though these are earlier in date.

From the plan and from comparative material elsewhere it is therefore possible to form an idea of the appearance of Jerusalem. We are fortunately in a better position concerning other towns of the Solomonic period. We still do not know much about most of the towns and villages of his kingdom, for though a dating to this period has been suggested for building phases in a number of sites, for instance Beth-shan and Beth-shemesh, the evidence is not yet very precise. There is, however, a group of cities especially associated with Solomon, which can be called his Royal Cities: Hazor, Megiddo and Gezer. They are specifically associated with his work in Jerusalem. In I Kings 9: 15 (New English Bible version) it is stated: 'This is the record of the forced labour which King Solomon conscripted to build the house of the Lord, his own palace, the Millo, the wall of Jerusalem, and Hazor, Megiddo and Gezer'.

These cities were strategically sited to command important areas and routes throughout the kingdom. Hazor lay in the Jordan valley, in the rich country between the Sea of Galilee and Lake Huleh, on the route to Damascus. Megiddo commanded the rich and fertile Plain of Esdraelon and, equally important, the pass over the neck of the Carmel range which was the most convenient route from Egypt to north Syria. Gezer lay at the foot of the hill country commanding the same route as it passed along the coastal plain and also commanded an important road from Jerusalem down to the coast. All had been powerful Canaanite towns but had suffered an eclipse; Solomon virtually refounded them. The destruction of Hazor in the thirteenth century BC has already been described. Megiddo was destroyed about 1100 BC and was possibly unoccupied for a hundred years. I Kings 9 describes a destruction of Gezer

54 Ivory bed-head from Nimrud, composed of ten panels with bearded warriors holding magical trees

55 Open-work ivory plaque from Nimrud. A pair of winged female figures wearing the Egyptian double crown protect with their outstretched wings the aegis of Bastet on a flowering 'lily' tree between them

56 Plan of the two palaces at Sendchirli (*after* Ussishkin)

by the Egyptian Pharaoh, who then gave it to Solomon as a dowry with his daughter. All three cities one might therefore say in modern jargon were 'ripe for redevelopment'.

Some of the most important contributions of recent archaeology to the illustration of the Bible concern these three cities. The excavation of Megiddo was carried out by the Oriental Institute of Chicago between 1925 and 1939. Reference is made in *The Bible and Archaeology* to the finds of the Solomonic period, especially to the 'Stables of Solomon', but recent research has shown the need for a complete reinterpretation. Hazor was first identified in 1875 and soundings were made by Professor John Garstang in 1928. Excavations on a very large scale, with spectacular results, were carried out between 1955 and 1958 by the James A. de Rothschild Expedition under the direction of Professor Yigael Yadin. Gezer had been extensively excavated between 1902 and 1909 on behalf of the Palestine Exploration Fund by Professor R. A. S. Macalister, but excavation methods then were primitive, and the true history of the site was only established by an expedition of the American Hebrew Union College school in Jerusalem under Dr W. Dever from 1964 to 1974. For all of the three cities, therefore, there has been a great growth of information in the last thirty-five years.

The Canaanite Hazor of the second millennium BC was an enormous place, with a Lower City forming a plateau of 175 acres added in the Middle Bronze Age onto an original Early Bronze mound; the Upper City covered at its

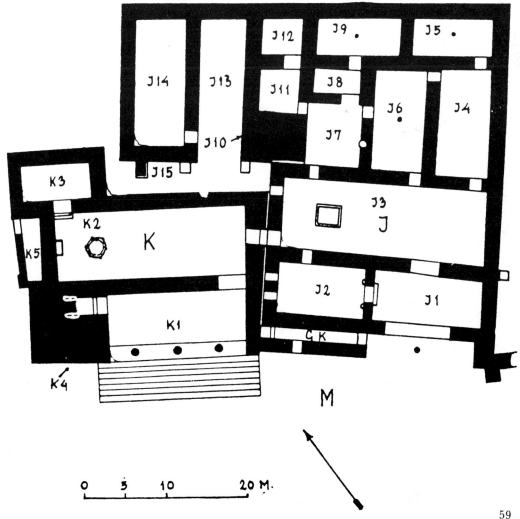

base 26 acres and at its summit 15 acres. The destruction in the thirteenth century BC involved both the Upper and Lower Cities, and the Lower City was never rebuilt. In due course the site was re-occupied by settlers with a completely different, non-urban, culture. They seem to have built no real houses and the only traces of them are the floors of huts or tents, fireplaces and a great number of storage pits. The associated pottery is twelfth century BC and the new inhabitants can be recognised as semi-nomadic tribesmen of the early stages of the Israelite infiltration. This first re-occupation was followed on the tell by a small, un-walled, village, in which the only important building may have been a cult centre.

The buildings that can be attributed to Solomon constitute the first return of Hazor to urban status. The area covered is small, consisting only of the western half of the original Upper City, the tell, but the lay-out was imposing. The chief feature was a defensive casemate wall, a form of double wall linked by cross walls, which enclosed the western end of the tell and cut this off from the eastern end by a line crossing the centre (57, 58). In the centre of this wall was an elaborate gateway with external towers and an entrance through three successive guard chambers. Only the foundations of the gateway and of most of the casemate wall survive, but there is no doubt that they form part of an elaborate and well-planned lay-out. The associated pottery shows that this lay-out can be dated to the mid-tenth century BC, and is therefore to be attributed to Solomon. Not much of the contemporary buildings within the town has been excavated, and there is no evidence that the imposing public buildings of the ninth century had Solomonic predecessors. One must, however, suppose that Solomon maintained a garrison in such a well fortified town, and the one building excavated in detail may perhaps be identified as a barracks.

It was immediately apparent to Professor Yadin that the plan of the Hazor gate was virtually identical with that of the inner Stratum V gate at Megiddo; Hazor, however, did not have the outer gateway guarding the approach up the side of the mound. As recorded by the excavators, however, this

Megiddo gateway was associated with a solid wall, built with a series of off-sets and insets. Professor Yadin was able to show, in a site c. 75 m. to the east of the gate that beneath the offsets and insets wall there was another with a casemate plan. Though the junction of this wall with the gate has not been proved, it is highly probable.

Portions of the Megiddo gate were much better preserved than were the defences at Hazor. It can therefore be established that the gate (59, 60), at least, was built of excellently dressed ashlar (61), in the Phoenician style found at Samaria, to which reference has been made in connection with Jerusalem.

It is now possible also at Megiddo to identify other structures that belong to the Solomonic period (62). In Yadin's excavations, the newly-discovered casemate wall abutted to the east and west against a building of imposing dimensions, of which the north wall formed part of the defences. The building, to which the name of Palace 6000 was given, was not completely excavated, but the plan was traced sufficiently to show that it resembled that of the palaces at Sendchirli, another parallel to Solomon's palace at Jerusalem.

Still more impressive was Palace 1723 (63), which can now be confidently ascribed to the time of Solomon. When the solid wall with offsets and insets was considered to be Solomonic, there was the difficulty that this building had been destroyed by the wall, and the building had either to be ascribed to David or to an early Solomonic phase, both very improbable. It had been destroyed to the top of its foundations, but a few ashlar blocks of the superstructure remained. Its plan can again be interpreted on the lines of the north Syrian palaces, with an entrance porch in room H, leading into an audience hall in room K, and the private quarters surrounding a courtyard, A.

Palace 1723 was set in a wide courtyard, entered through a projecting porch, in which courses of bossed Phoenician masonry survived. The enclosure wall of the courtyard also contained ashlar blocks of Phoenician type, employed as piers in walls built of rough rubble. The ashlars in these walls are, however, certainly re-used. The courtyard must have been

57 Air view of the Solomonic gate at Hazor

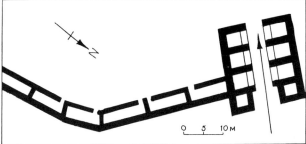

58 Plan of the Solomonic gate at Hazor (*after* Yadin)

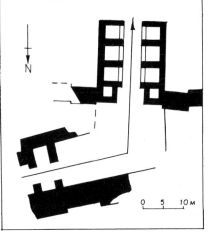

59 Plan of the Solomonic gate at Megiddo (*after* Yadin)

60 View of the Solomonic gate at
Megiddo

61 Detail of the masonry of the
door jamb of the Solomonic gate at
Megiddo

62 Plan of Solomonic Megiddo

rebuilt at the same time as the so-called Stables, in similar style masonry, were constructed. To these buildings we will return. Adjacent to the Palace 1723 complex was another impressive structure, 1482, which belongs to the same layout.

A further important element which Yadin has shown belongs to the Solomonic period is the covered gallery leading to the spring at the foot of the mound. This gallery then passes beneath the offsets and insets wall, but since it had been proved that this wall was not Solomonic, it is no longer necessary to push the gallery back into the Canaanite period. The facing of the walls of the gallery was in fact of typical Phoenician-type ashlars, and excavation showed that it was cut through the same layers, strata VIA and VB as were cut by Palace 6000; it can thus safely be ascribed to Solomon.

The picture of Solomonic Megiddo has therefore changed radically since *The Bible and Archaeology* was written in 1940. The Samaria excavations provided pottery evidence to prove that the 'Solomonic Stables' were not Solomonic, and showed what Phoenician-inspired masonry looked like. The Hazor excavations provided the essential key to the lay-out of a Solomonic town. As a result, Megiddo is now the best documented of Solomon's royal cities, and we have some conception of what Jerusalem may have looked like. Megiddo was certainly dominated by imposing public buildings. What we still cannot say is what the rest of the area enclosed by the casemate walls looked like. The Chicago excavations recorded as the next stratum beneath IV, that of the 'Solomonic Stables', the very undistinguished little buildings of VA. When the evidence of the true Solomonic buildings was emerging it seemed possible that there were grand official buildings inserted into the setting of old-fashioned private dwellings. A further point brought to light by Yadin's excavations suggests that there may have been a stage between VA and IV which was completely missed by the earlier excavators. This was that to the south of Palace 6000, and separated from it by a street ten metres wide, was a very large building of which almost the only evi-

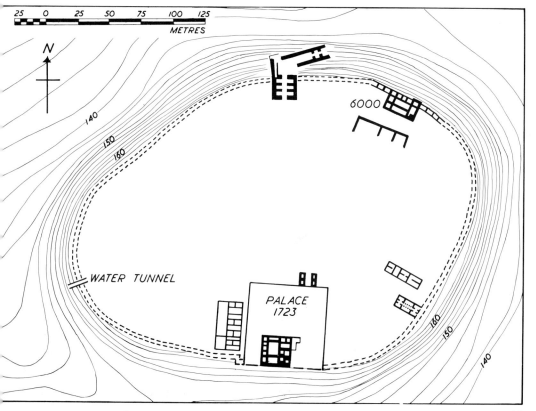

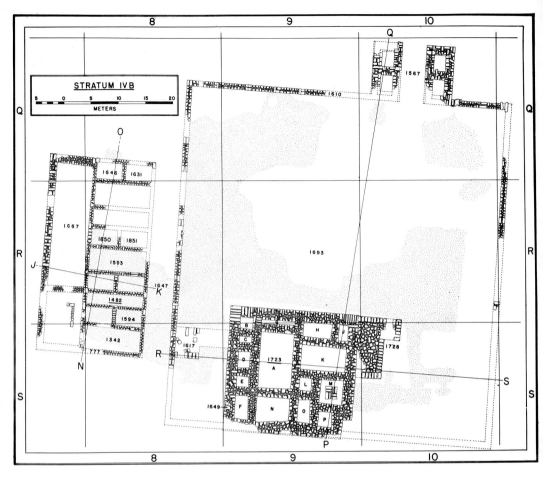

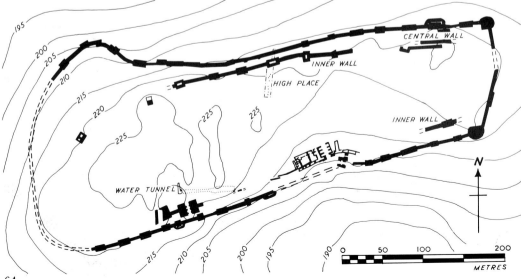

63 Plan of Palace 1723 at Megiddo

64 Plan of Gezer

64

dence was provided by robber trenches which had removed the stones from the walls for re-use elsewhere, but left the floors intact to show the line that walls had followed; much of the lay-out of the Omri and Ahab buildings at Samaria had been traced in the same way. Such evidence would certainly have been missed in the excavation methods of the earlier excavations, and for the time being there is therefore uncertainty as to the extent of the Solomonic buildings. Certainly the number of re-used ashlars in the stratum IV buildings would suggest a very considerable pillaging of earlier structures.

The third of the cities referred to in the I Kings text is Gezer. This was excavated even earlier than Megiddo, between 1902 and 1909, with very much more primitive methods. The plan published then suggested to Professor Yadin that in the structures designated 'the Maccabean Castle' there could be identified parts of a casemate wall and a gateway of the same plan as those of Hazor and Megiddo. The pier of the gateway, moreover, was in the fine, flat-dressed ashlars of the best Phoenician-type masonry (65, 66). This identification has been triumphantly proved by the American Hebrew Union College excavations of 1964 to 1974. In these excavations, the gate complex was shown to be identical with that of Megiddo, except

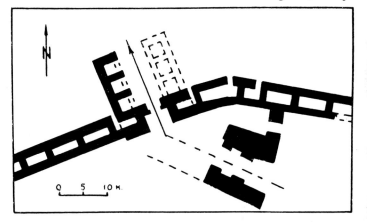

65 Plan of the Solomonic gate at Gezer (*after* Yadin)

66 Detail of the masonry of the Solomonic gate at Gezer

that the outer gateway and approach road was from the right (looking at the inner gate) instead of from the left as at Megiddo. A deep drain (67) runs through the centre of the gate passage; this belongs to a reconstruction and must have been covered, probably in wood. The gate was founded on an artifical terrace, constructed of debris derived from a preceding destruction. The finds were early tenth century BC in date, and can confidently be linked to the passage in I Kings 9 describing how Pharaoh, probably Siamun, the penultimate king of the Twenty-first Dynasty, had burnt Gezer to the ground, put its Canaanite inhabitants to death and given it to Solomon as a dowry for his daughter. Once again, the Biblical narrative is excellently illustrated by the archaeological evidence.

The recent excavations only traced a short length of the casemate wall associated with the gate. The excavators believe it was built as a blocking of a gap in the outer wall (64), but I would suggest that an alternative interpretation can be put forward. The outer wall seems more likely to be Maccabean, with towers added to it which made use of Solomonic ashlars, and these activities of the Maccabean builders could have accounted for the disappearance of much of the Solomonic wall, though a section of it on the north side was in fact found by Macalister. Nothing of the rest of the Solomonic city was recovered. The evidence for it may well have been, as at Megiddo, simply robber trenches, which would not have been observed in the 1902-09 excavations.

Solomon had thus transformed the face of Israelite Palestine, and probably the way of life of many of its inhabitants. The principal towns had a very different aspect from the ordinary Canaanite towns and villages into which the Israelite tribesmen had infiltrated, and which they had gradually taken over. The evidence just described concerns Solomon's principal towns, but I Kings 9: 18-19 refers in addition to his building at 'Lower Beth-horon, Baalath and Tamar in the wilderness, as well as all his store-cities, and the towns where he quartered his chariots and horses'. Official buildings and central administration must therefore have made a considerable impact throughout the kingdom.

67 View of the Solomonic gate at Gezer with a drain of a secondary stage passing through the centre

5 The Archaeological Evidence for the Period of the Divided Monarchy of Judah and Israel

he growth of the central power of the monarchy clearly had its opponents among the tribally-minded Israelites. Hitherto the tribes had been held together by the brilliance, personality and success of David and Solomon, but almost immediately after Solomon's death in 925 BC the old antagonism between the northern and southern tribes re-asserted itself, and the north broke away to form the kingdom of Israel. Of Solomon's great cities, only Jerusalem remained to Judah.

Though the northern tribes broke away from Solomon's son Rehoboam in protest against the exactions of the central government, archaeological evidence shows that it was in the northern kingdom that royal luxury and the trappings of central government continued to flourish. It was in fact inevitable that Judah should become the poor relation. The agricultural land lay in Israel, with much of Judah poor hill country or semi-desert. Israel, moreover, could trade freely by land or sea with the rest of western Asia, whereas Judah was encircled by unfriendly countries with which she was often at war.

The northern kingdom was at first without a capital. The Biblical account shows that the breakaway king, Jeroboam, first made Shechem his capital and then Penuel. It is only in the course of several dynastic changes, all involving much bloodshed, that the capital was established at Tirzah, and it was there that Omri, the founder of a new and powerful dynasty, established his rule.

The identification of Tirzah is a nice contribution of archaeology to history. The site of Tell el Far'ah (N.) (68) lies on the east side of the mountains of Ephraim in the Wadi Far'ah which runs down into the Jordan valley. Excavations have shown that it was an important town in the Early Bronze Age and again in the Middle and Late Bronze Ages. It was one of the places which authorities such as Professor Albright had suggested might be Tirzah. The proof came from the excavations of Père Roland de Vaux which began in 1946.

The literary clue comes from the statement in I Kings 16: 23-24 that Omri, after having reigned six years in Tirzah, then transferred his capital to Samaria, where he likewise reigned six years. The date of the transfer was probably c. 878 BC, though an alternative chronology would make it c. 886 BC. The site of Samaria is well known (69), and the latest excavations carried out there by a joint British, American and Hebrew University expedition between 1931 and 1935 identified the Omri buildings on the virgin site that the Biblical account leads us to expect. 'He bought the hill of Samaria from Shemer for two talents of silver and built a city on it which he named Samaria after Shemer the owner of the hill' (I Kings 16: 24). The excavations showed that the only occupation that preceded Omri's city belonged to the Chalcolithic period in the fourth millennium BC, and thereafter the hill lay vacant. The pottery and other finds associated with the new buildings belonged to those brought to the site by Omri to construct his new city, and these builders, on the Biblical evidence, would have been brought from Tirzah. De Vaux's excavations showed that the Tell el Far'ah site continued to be an important city until well into the Iron Age. Then there is a sudden break, with an interregnum in which there was very slight occupation. The pottery of the last Tell el Far'ah phase before this break corresponds with the first Iron Age pottery to appear at Samaria, and that associated with the succeeding early phases at Samaria is missing at Tell el Far'ah. The fit is perfect. Omri transferred his capital to Samaria and took with him most of the inhabitants of his first capital. There is even an unfinished lay-out at Far'ah, suggesting that Omri had started to redesign Tirzah before deciding to move elsewhere.

Omri's reason for the move was partly geographical. Tirzah in the Wadi Far'ah was in something of a backwater, looking east across the Jordan, and cut off from main lines of communication. Samaria lay on the main north-south highway. The modern road skirts its foot, and the ancient one was not far away. Contact and trade with Phoenicia to the north and Damascus and the whole of north Syria and Mesopotamia to the north-east was easy, and the Mediterranean was visible to the west.

It may have been equally important to Omri to have a free hand in building a capital worthy of his status in relation to his neighbours to the north. A virgin site like the hill of Samaria gave him this freedom which the built-up town of Tirzah did not provide. What he did was to take the whole of the summit of the hill for a royal quarter. In fact, we do not know where the ordinary people lived, since excavations have been concentrated on the summit (70). A brief and limited excavation in 1967 showed that there was no lower town on the northern slopes, and it is probable that the private houses must have lain to the east, beneath the modern village of Sebaste.

The essence of Omri's plan was an enclosure wall surrounding a courtyard in which were set his palace and his administrative buildings. The summit of the hill of Samaria is gently rounded, but some terracing was necessary to provide space for the courtyard. The enclosure wall was therefore also a retaining wall. Most of our evidence concerning the appearance of Omri's buildings comes from the enclosure wall, fortunately buried when his son Ahab slightly extended the summit courtyard with an encircling casemate wall. Some part of what was probably the actual palace does survive, but for the most part the buildings within the courtyard have been robbed of their stones and the plans can only be traced by the robber trenches.

8 Air view of Tell el Far'ah

9 View of Samaria

10 Plan of the royal quarter of Samaria, surrounded by the casemate wall with, inside it, an earlier wall shown in fig. 71

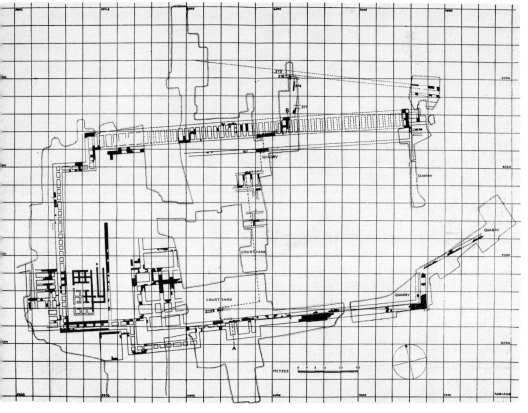

The fragments of wall that do survive, however, suggest the excellent quality of the workmanship both in Omri's original buildings and those of Ahab which followed probably without interval. Slighter walls were built of flat-dressed ashlar blocks with an exactness of fitting that can only be described as exquisite (71). Heavier walls had finely dressed marginal drafts, but were given an appearance of massive strength by irregularly protruding bosses (72). The Phoenician character of this masonry can be firmly established by comparison with surviving buildings in that area. It was very natural that Omri should follow Solomon's example in borrowing Phoenician craftsmen, for his son Ahab had married a Phoenician princess, Jezabel. The Samaria excavations were the first to identify this type of masonry in Palestine. From this evidence we can suggest what Solomon's buildings in Jerusalem looked like, and identify firmly as his work similar walls at Megiddo and Gezer (61, 66).

The other major contribution of the Samaria excavations that helps one to visualise the appearance of towns of the Old Testament period was the discovery of ivory carvings. The epitaph of Ahab, the second king to rule at Samaria, as recorded in I Kings 22 : 39 includes 'the ivory house which he built'. The ivory carvings found in the excavations were on a small scale, and had ornamented furniture rather than a house, but a lavish provision of furniture thus decorated could well have given this name to Ahab's palace. Our increased knowledge of the use of ivory carvings as the result of excavations at Nimrud in Assyria has already been mentioned in connection with Jerusalem.

It was in the northern kingdom of Israel, therefore, that we find the full development of cities dominated by the king's administrative centre. The virgin site of Samaria gave Omri the chance of designing a new city on these lines. One can deduce such a centre in Solomonic Jerusalem, and at Megiddo there were certainly important official buildings at this time, but much of the evidence has been destroyed. It is from the secondary stratum at Megiddo that one can obtain the clearest idea of the lay-out of such a centre. Solomonic Megiddo may have been severely damaged in

the raid of Shishak I of Egypt in c. 922-921 BC If that is the case it must have remained in state of disarray for nearly three-quarters of century, for the pottery evidence shows that th rebuilding was not completed until the time of Samaria Period III, about the middle of th ninth century; probably political power in th Northern Kingdom was too shaky for majo rebuildings until the Omrid dynasty was firm on the throne.

When the rebuilding at Megiddo came, was grandiose (73). The summit was encircle by a new wall and it looks as if the whole summ of the mound was occupied by imposing publ buildings. The new wall contrasts with that of Solomon in that it is not built with casemat but is solid, with inner and outer faces bui with shallow insets and offsets. The plan of th Solomonic gateway was retained, but its leve was raised to the extent of some 2.25 m. Nothin of the superstructure of the new gate survive For the most part, the new wall followed th line of its predecessor, except that where th casemate wall had abutted on two palace 6000 in the north and 1723 in the south, th new wall continued straight across and abo ished these buildings. The whole 6000 comple was abolished. In the case of 1723, the actu palace building was abolished, but the cour yard wall was, as will be seen, rebuilt, an there may have been a new building within i for which the much-disturbed strata did n provide evidence.

The most striking new buildings were wha the excavators called 'Solomon's Stables'. Th publication of the Samaria architectural an pottery evidence long ago proved that the were not Solomonic, and it can now be doubte whether they were really stables. A fin confirmation that the stables were n Solomonic was Professor Yadin's discovery tha beneath the northern stables lay the Solomon palace 6000. The biggest 'stable' comple which had attached to it a large courtyar 55 m. square, was on the south side of th summit, and abolished part of the buildin adjoining palace 1723. The interpretation these buildings as stables by the excavato seemed convincing. They consisted of a numb of units of tripartite plan. A central alleyw was divided by rows of stone pillars from ston

71 Detail of the masonry of the Period I
wall at Samaria with Period III wall on left

72 Wall with bossed masonry at
Samaria

73 Plan of Stratum IV at Megiddo

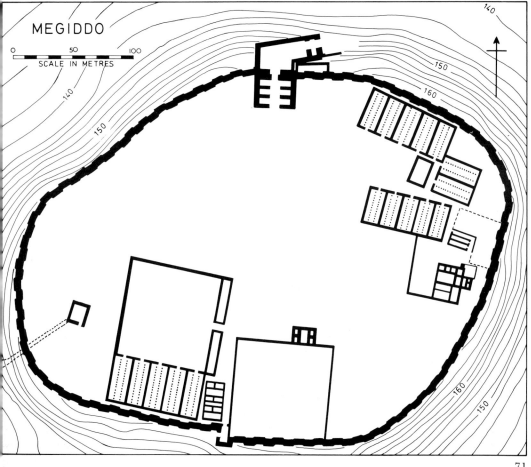

MEGIDDO

0   50   100
SCALE IN METRES

paved side galleries (74). Between many of the pillars were stone troughs, which would have served as mangers. The side galleries would have been the stalls, the central alleyway a service area. It is, however, odd that the stone troughs, 0.70 m. high, form a continuous boundary between the stalls and the central alleyway, except in the case of the section next to the entrance. The horses could therefore have been taken out only as complete units, regardless of the needs of individual horses, which would seem to be a cumbersome procedure. Modern horse-owners, moreover, would not like the idea of an undivided stall area, in which a restless or vicious horse could severely injure its neighbours. There could have been wooden divisions, but there is nothing in structure or floor wear to suggest it.

The main reason for querying the interpretation of the buildings as stables, however, is that buildings identical in plan at Hazor and Beersheba are interpreted differently. At Beersheba the buildings were found stacked with pottery, and were certainly used as stores. As far as Megiddo is concerned, the question must remain open. It is presumably not impos-

sible that a standard structural plan could serve different purposes.

The other point of note about these buildings is the method of construction. Of the stable units themselves, almost nothing of the super-structure survives, but there is more evidence concerning the wall that enclosed the courtyard of the southern stables. In this, there was a series of piers of ashlars with, between the piers, walls of rough, undressed stones. The same method was employed in the courtyard surrounding the site of the Solomonic palace 1723 (63). The ashlars immediately suggest comparison with the Omri walls at Samaria. Examination, however, makes it abundantly clear that stones are re-used, with chipped edges and badly fitting joints. Their source, no doubt, was the ruins of the Solomonic buildings; it has already been mentioned above that some of the walls of these buildings could be traced only by the robber trenches, and almost nothing of any of them survives above ground level.

The lay-out of the summit of the town of Megiddo in the time of the Divided Monarchy consisted of impressive public buildings.

Between them, in the light of the evidence of slightly earlier Samaria, were probably open courtyards. The other great construction belonging to this period was a new approach to the water-source. There were too many potential enemies for a site like Megiddo not to be provided with safe access to its water supply. The Solomonic approach was by means of a long gallery (p. 63); its successor was a more ambitious affair, providing access to the spring which could be much more safely protected from the outside. It consisted of a shaft 35 m. deep, cut partly through the earlier occupation layers and partly through solid rock with, at its base, a rock-cut tunnel 63 m. long (75, 76).

Megiddo was therefore remodelled in the mid-ninth century, perhaps following a period of decay after the Shishak destruction, on the model of the new capital of the Northern Kingdom, Omri's and Ahab's Samaria. Hazor provides the same evidence. The Solomonic town, with its casemate walls, had only included the western end of the mound which had grown up in the Early Bronze Age, to which the enormous outer city had been added during the Middle Bronze Age. In the first half of the

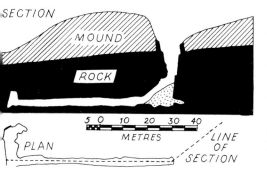

75 Plan and section of the water shaft at Megiddo

74 View of the so-called 'Solomonic stables' at Megiddo

76 The tunnel to the spring cut through the rock at Megiddo

73

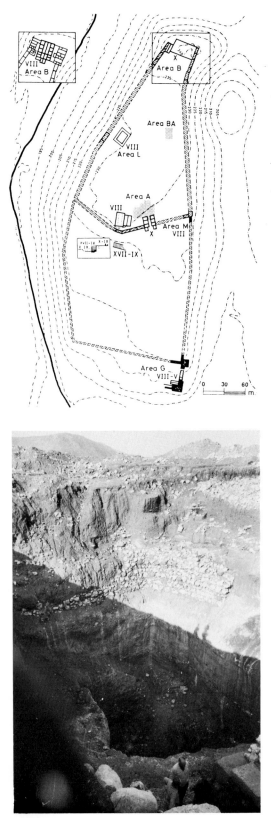

ninth century BC, and ascribed to Ahab, the defences were extended some 180 m. to the east, to enclose the whole of the original mound. The new wall was solid, and the Solomonic casemate angle at the west end was filled in to convert it into the new type of structure. The defences were further strengthened by the construction of a massive citadel at the west end, where the top of the mound narrowed almost to a point (77). Another public building had a tripartite plan divided by two rows of stone pillars, similar in plan to the Megiddo 'stables'. The evidence at Hazor, however, indicated that the building was used for storage, with compartments between the pillars containing storage jars and craters.

A further link with ninth-century Megiddo is the discovery of a very similar watershaft (78, 79). This was, as at Megiddo, cut through earlier strata at the top, and below through solid rock. The excavator, Professor Yadin, was fortunately well aware of the necessity of observing the date of the layers through which the shaft cut, and there was excellent evidence that the shaft was later than the Solomonic casemate wall. The total depth of the shaft was *c*. 30 m., whereas the direct shaft at Megiddo was *c*. 25 m. to the point at which originally steps descended to a tunnel 63 m. long. At Hazor, steps sloped down direct to the water pool. The most surprising thing about the Hazor water system is that the engineers concerned realised that they did not have to cut their tunnel outside the walls to tap the visible springs in the adjacent valley, and that they would be able to reach the water level at a point safely within the defences. In this respect, they were superior to their contemporaries at Megiddo.

At Samaria, the summit of the hill remained a royal quarter throughout the ninth and eighth centuries BC. Rebuildings contemporary with the mid-ninth century lay-outs at Hazor and Megiddo, just described, can be identified, but the capital did not require the extensive redesigning of the other sites, for which it had provided the planning model. The main interest of the new buildings and rebuildings at Samaria is the emphasis it places on the distinction between the Phoenician-style masonry found in Omri's and Ahab's buildings and the native style that re-appears in the subsequent building periods. This is clearly shown where a Period II rebuilding overlies the original Omri wall. It is the same phenomenon that is seen, for instance, at Megiddo, where the fine ashlars of the Solomonic buildings are re-used in the rough walls of the mid-ninth century rebuilding. The Israelites could plan impressively, but they were not apt pupils in mason's work.

The rebuilding of the Solomonic Royal Cities as administrative centres with imposing official buildings seems to have been confined to the northern kingdom of Israel. In this area, excavations are also revealing important public buildings at Dan. Nothing comparable has been found at Gezer, the third city associated with Solomon, though admittedly there are large unexcavated areas. Excavation has, however, given us much greater knowledge of the smaller towns of the kingdom of Judah than we possess about Israel. This may correctly illustrate a difference in development between the two kingdoms.

There are quite a number of towns within Judah where excavations have produced detailed plans. All are defended by substantial town walls because Judah was so small and so encircled by potential enemies that the inhab-

itants had to be ready to defend themselves. The plan of Tell Beersheba (80), gives an idea of the lay-out of such places. Since, however, the plan gives prominence to large storehouses, the site may correspond as an administrative centre with the larger centres in Israel. The use of these pillared halls for storage was very clearly demonstrated by the finds in them. The general layout, with structures built radially against the town walls and separated by a ring road from the main block of houses in the centre of the town, can be paralleled in a number of other sites, for instance at Tell Beit Mirsim.

The nearest equivalent in Judah to the royal cities of the northern kingdom is probably to be found in a number of citadels along the southern borders, forming a line of defence against the occupants of the semi-desert area to the south and against invaders from across the Jordan. The best known example is Arad, where a strongly defended citadel was established on part of a site that had been an important city in the fourth and early third millennia. The necessity for such strong points is emphasised by the fact that there were six successive building phases of the citadel from

7 Plan of the upper city at Hazor (after Yadin)

8 The entrance to the water shaft at Hazor

9 Plan of the water shaft at Hazor (after Yadin)

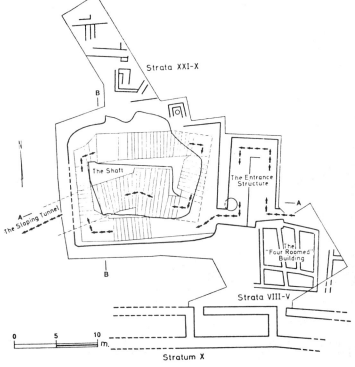

the time of Solomon down to the seventh century BC; each in turn destroyed by fire, presumably as the result of enemy attack. An interesting point is that all the citadels except the latest contained a sanctuary associated with the worship of Yahweh. The sanctuary may have been abolished during the religious reforms of Josiah in the seventh century BC.

Another surprising piece of evidence for religious practices in Judah comes from the capital itself. Even Jerusalem, the centre of the worship of Yahweh, provides an illustration of the influence of the heathen Canaanite fertility cults which the infiltrating Israelite tribes had found established, and which for centuries' continued to attract them. The epitaph of many of the kings, particularly those of Israel, was 'and he did what was evil in the sight of the Lord and went after false gods'. At a distance of only about 300 m. from the platform of the

Temple of Yahweh, low on the eastern slope of Jerusalem and just outside the town wall a sanctuary of such a heathen cult was found in the 1961-7 excavations (81). It consisted of a small room containing two standing stones *mazzeboth,* almost certainly to be interpreted as cult objects, with, above a rock scarp, the foundations of an altar (82). A door in the *mazzeboth* room enabled libations to be poured at the foot of the scarp beneath the altar. Adjoining the *mazzeboth* room was a cave that served as a repository for vessels that must have contained offerings at the sanctuary, similar in purpose to the pits that surrounded the Lachish Temple some 800 years earlier. Another larger cave near by, associated with the same or an adjacent sanctuary, contained hundreds of vessels, figurines of the mother-goddess type and horses with disks between the ears, perhaps models of Horses of the Sun.

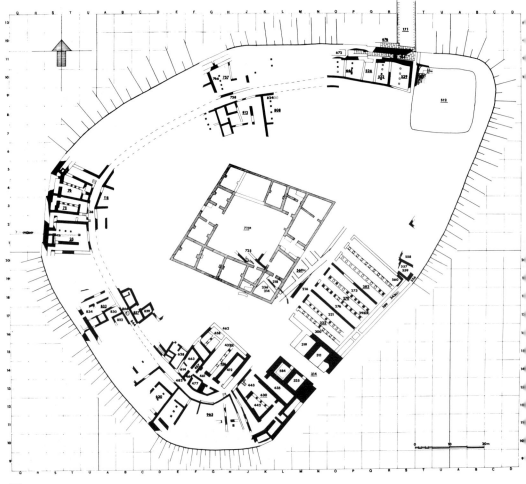

81 View of excavations on the east slopes of Jerusalem with the site of the cult centre (seen in detail below) to the right of the dumps of the main trench

80 Plan of Tell Beersheba (*after* Aharoni). The central building is a Roman fortress

82 The Jerusalem cult centre with, in the background on the scarp, the probable altar. Below centre, the *mazzeboth* and, to the left, the cave for discarded vessels which had contained offerings

Archaeology has thus built up a fairly detailed picture of life in the settlements of the period of the historical books of the Bible, particularly during the period of the divided Monarchy. Emphasis is of course on the larger settlements, for they reveal the most interesting remains. The evidence at present suggests that the bulk of the population was concentrated in the walled towns and villages. This may in fact be because small villages do not advertise themselves by surface remains, and have therefore escaped notice. In a country as interested in archaeology as the modern state of Israel, this is not very likely. It is quite reasonable to accept that in times in which war and threats of war were never far away the majority of the inhabitants preferred to live behind defences, in sizeable groups.

The troubles threatening the inhabitants of Judah and Israel from the tenth to the eighth centuries BC were those of wars between adjacent states of reasonably equal strength. For most of this period neither Egypt nor a Mesopotamiam power was strong enough to have imperial ambitions in western Asia. This position changed with the rise to power of Assyria in the second half of the eighth century. The second book of Kings tells us of the disasters which struck the northern kingdom in the reigns of Pekah (II Kings 15: 29) and Hoshea (II Kings 17: 6), in which in two stages Israel was overwhelmed, the inhabitants exiled and their place taken by captives transferred from other parts of the Assyrian Empire. This is the disappearance of the Ten Tribes, the lost tribes, which became merged with the inhabitants of adjoining countries and lost their identity as Israelites. So, too, did any who were not sent into captivity, for they were so submerged by the newcomers that the inhabitants of Judah never accepted the Samaritans as of true Jewish blood.

Archaeology has provided ample evidence to support the Biblical account. Of the first stage, when the northern part of the kingdom of Israel was lost, the excavations at Hazor have provided the best evidence. Hazor had suffered severely from an earthquake, probably in 760 BC. The succeeding stratum V was the last Israelite fortified city, and was rebuilt immediately after the earthquake on much the same plan as its predecessor. The main differenc was in some strengthening of the defences due no doubt, to awareness of the aggressive plan of Assyria. Vivid evidence of the capture o Hazor by the Assyrians in 732 BC was provide by a thick layer of ashes all over the stratum V buildings and the virtual disappearance of th town. For a short period there were some poo structures over the ruins, which were soo superseded by a citadel which remained as military and administrative centre down t about 400 BC. Round it grew up some farm houses, but Hazor as a town disappeared.

Megiddo suffered a similar fate in this firs Assyrian invasion of Israel. The town wa subsequently rebuilt, on a completely differen plan, and remained in existence as a tow down to about the fourth century BC.

There was a short lull in Assyrian attacks due to dynastic troubles at home, before th rest of the kingdom of Israel was obliterated Archaeology amply confirms the destruction o Samaria, at a date which can be historicall fixed as 722 BC, by Sargon II after a three-yea siege begun by Shalmaneser V. The roya quarter on the summit of the hill that had bee established by Omri c. 880 BC had continue to exist, with additions gradually filling in part of the spacious courtyards, though the architec ture and masonry showed a steady decline i standards. A find in one of these buildings o records of dues and taxes collected, written i ink on potsherds, gives confirmation of the us of this area for official administration, and glimpse of the administrative methods em ployed. All this comes to a complete end wit the Assyrian attack. The whole of the are excavated was found covered with a thick laye of ashes, and the buildings on the summit wer destroyed to ground level. In the ashes wer found some of the ivories that had decorate the furniture in the palace of Ahab. In th overlying layers were sherds of a new style o pottery certainly derived from Assyrian proto types, and which is also found elsewhere in th area of the northern kingdom captured at thi time, for instance at Tirzah and Shechem, an also in the coastal area included in a wid sweep of Assyrian conquests at this stage.

The archaeological evidence of the fall of th kingdom of Israel is almost more vivid tha hat of the Biblical record. In II Kings 17: 6 it ates 'In the ninth year of Hoshea the king of ssyria captured Samaria, and he carried the sraelites away to Assyria, and placed them in lalah, and on the Habor, the river of Gozan, nd in the cities of the Medes'. In verses 7 to 17 ll the sins of the inhabitants of the northern ingdom against Yahweh are dramatically sted. Verse 18 reads 'And the Lord rejected all he descendants of Israel, and afflicted them, nd gave them into the hand of spoilers until he ad cast them out of his sight'. One might have suspicion that some of this is hyperbole, the esult of hostility between the kingdoms of udah, to which the writer belongs, and Israel. he complete obliteration of the Israelite towns f Samaria and Hazor and the accompanying estruction of Megiddo is the factual archaeo- ogical evidence that the writer was not xaggerating.

A possible reflection in Jerusalem of these events in the northern kingdom was the exten- sion of the city onto the western ridge. The archaeological evidence is clear that at the time of Solomon only the eastern ridge, with the Temple at its northern end, was defended. At some period before the end of the monarchy, part of the western ridge was enclosed, probably forming the Mishneh, or Second Quarter. Excavations since 1967 within the area of the Old City have revealed houses of the eighth- seventh century BC and a length of very massive town wall. The exact date is not yet precisely fixed, but it is a very reasonable suggestion that it was to accomodate refugees from the north. The line of this wall is also not certain. The evidence of the 1961-7 excavations shows that it did not extend to the summit of the western ridge, nor enclose the eastern slope of the western ridge to join the southern tip of the

3 Plan of Jerusalem during the ater monarchy

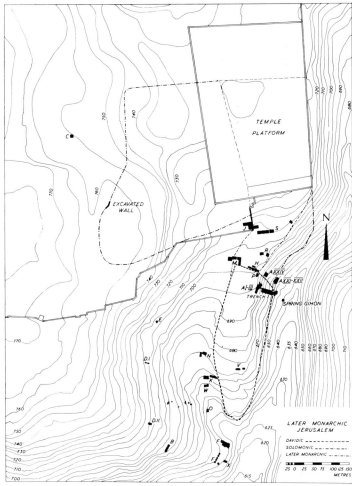

original town, though this is the line preferred by the Israeli archaeologists. A suggested plan (83) is feasible, though an extension further south on the upper slopes of the ridge, giving a more developed two-pronged outline, would be quite possible.

It could be that the immediate effect of the Assyrian conquests at Jerusalem was an increase in size; but the kingdom of Judah might with reason expect a fate similar to that of its neighbour.

The next stage of Assyrian advance came under Sennacherib about 705 BC. Many towns in Judah fell to him, and the capture of the important town of Lachish is depicted in reliefs found in his palace at Nineveh. An Assyrian helmet, crest and scales of armour have been found at Tell Duweir, identified as the site of Lachish, though it is probable that the destruction of Level III belongs not here but to the sixth century.

Jerusalem was saved by Hezekiah's diplomacy and active measures of defence. Excavations on the east slope of the original city show that the original wall of the Jebusites with its Davidic and Solomonic repairs was superseded during the late eighth century by a succession of others, which enclosed the lower slopes to the north that had been outside the Solomonic city (83). One of these walls was probably the work of Hezekiah. A still more remarkable testimony to the measures he took is the Siloam Tunnel. In II Chronicles 32: 3-4 it is stated, 'he planned with his officers and his mighty men to stop the water of the springs that were outside the city; and they helped him. A great many people were gathered, and they stopped all the springs and the brook that flowed through the land, saying, "Why should the kings of Assyria come and find much water?"' The reference in II Kings 20: 20 is to his construction of the pool and the conduit. It has long been accepted that this description refers to the Siloam Tunnel, through which the water from the Spring Gihon still runs. The tunnel passes beneath the ancient city and emerges into the Siloam Pool in the central valley near the southern tip of the eastern ridge. The 1961-7 excavations exposed the difficulties that this pool was outside the contemporary city, for there was clear evidence that the commanding slopes of the western ridge were undefended. The explanation is that the original pool was an underground, rock-cut cistern, accessible by a shaft or staircase from within the city, and invisible to attackers from outside.

Hezekiah's measures were sufficiently effective to delay the Assyrian army long enough for plague to attack it and cause a complete withdrawal. The kingdom of Judah was thus reprieved for a century, though it was effectively a vassal of Assyria and subsequently of Babylon, which in 626 BC achieved supremacy over Assyria.

84 An example of one of the Lachish letters written on a potsherd. It contains a list of Hebrew names

85 The rebuilt eastern wall of Jerusalem in the Late Monarchic period. The walls in the background are modern

At a considerable number of sites archaeology as provided testimony of the material culture the kingdom of Judah during this period, for he houses of the period were in due course uried beneath the ensuing destruction. Town nd village life flourished. Some places provided vidence of oil and wine making, others of yeing, and at Jerusalem the find of a collection f small weights suggests the shop of a jeweller. t no place is there any evidence of a high andard of architectural or building skills; ost houses were of roughly trimmed stone ith a covering of mud plaster. All in all, owever, it was a period of reasonable material rosperity.

The end of this phase in the life of the Jews mes with the renewed advance westward of e Mesopotamian power, now Babylon. Both Kings and II Chronicles provide the historical cord of the last desperate struggles of the lers of Judah to avoid annihilation, and the ook of Jeremiah records the background of ligious and political intrigues.

Archaeology provides vivid evidence of the results of the two Babylonian campaigns of 597 and 587 BC. Most of this evidence consists of utterly ruined towns and villages, with a virtually complete break in the old pattern of occupation. An exceptional piece of evidence is a group of ostraca, potsherds used for writing letters, found at Lachish (84). These were known when *Archaeology and the Bible* was written, but are referred to again here since they add much to the picture. They belong to a stage when most of Judah seems to have fallen to the invaders. The commander of an outpost near Lachish refers to the fact that he was dependent on signals from Lachish since 'we do not see Azekah'; this town, through which signals from Jerusalem would have reached him, must already have fallen. Other references are to a prophet, who may be Uriah, or even Jeremiah himself, whose escape this officer is apparently accused of abetting when he was opposing the royal policy. There is much in the letters of which the meaning is uncertain. In

86 Evidence of the Babylonian destruction of Jerusalem. The tumble of the top of the eastern slope envelops a seventh-century house

spite of that, a feeling of crisis and anxiety comes through dramatically. One could imagine scraps of correspondence in England in 1940 showing the same feeling. In 1940, the crisis was survived, but for the kingdom of Judah it ended in total disaster.

The kings of Judah in the last years of the seventh century BC tried to play off the revived power of Egypt against that of Babylon. Unfortunately they guessed wrong and suffered a grievous punishment for opposing Babylon. In 597 Jerusalem was destroyed and the Temple looted, but the city was not obliterated. The Jews had still not learnt their lesson, and a further revolt was followed by another Babylonian campaign. The walls of Jerusalem were strong enough to withstand a siege for eighteen months. A portion of these walls, in which many repairs can be traced still remains (85). Its strength lies in the fact that it is backed against a thick fill on the side of the hill and that it could only be attacked up a steep slope. In the event, it was famine that brought about the fall of the city and led to the attempted escape of King Zedekiah and his army to Jericho. The attempt was unsuccessful and Zedekiah ended his days as a prisoner in Babylon.

The 1961-7 excavations provided vivid evidence of the destruction of Jerusalem as the capital of the kingdom of Judah. The sack of the city is described in II Kings 25: 13, 14, and it was followed by the burning of the Temple and all the other public and important private buildings. The city wall was broken down (II Kings 25: 10) and as a result the intricate terrace system that on the east side interlocked with the city wall, the lowest element in the terracing, collapsed down the hill in a tumble of stones. This tumble is seen at the top of the slope, enveloping the seventh-century house founded on the Jebusite terrace there (86), and all down the east side of the last stage of Old Testament Jerusalem is represented by tumble of rubble up to 6 m. thick.

This collapse was the end of Jebusite and monarchical Jerusalem. All except the poorest in the land were taken away to exile in Babylon and the city lay in ruins. The group that was allowed by the Persians to return c. 530 BC rebuilt the Temple, but the walls were not rebuilt until Nehemiah was sent as Governor c. 440 BC. He found the eastern side in such complete ruin that he left the whole slope outside the city, and built his wall on the crest of the ridge.

6 New Testament Palestine

This chapter extends beyond the period of the New Testament and covers the period called by the Israelis the period of the Second Temple. This begins with the rebuilding of the Temple by Zerubbabel, finished c. 515 BC, and includes numerous repairs, even the complete reconstruction and enlargement carried out by Herod the Great. Hitherto, the divisions usually employed have been the Post-Exilic or Persian, the Hellenistic or Maccabean, the Herodian and Roman periods. Archaeology has not made any very striking contributions to the history of most of these periods. It was in Palestine a stage of gradual recuperation and reorganisation, first under Persian rule, then under competing Hellenistic powers, and ultimately with Rome taking an every-increasing direct control. For readers of the Bible, the next main period of interest is that of the New Testament. Palestine at that time was part of the Roman Empire, having been captured by Pompey in 63 BC. Something, however, must be said of the immediate background of the country thus Romanised.

As has been seen, there were differences between north and south at every stage in the history of Israel. These were very much accentuated by the events that ended the kingdoms of Israel and Judah. Israel fell to the Assyrians in the eighth century; Megiddo and Hazor c. 730, Samaria in 720 BC. A considerable part of the population was carried into exile and disappeared for ever, their place being taken by exiles from other parts of the Assyrian Empire. Thereafter, the inhabitants of the northern province were despised as not being of pure race. Jerusalem and most of Judah survived the Assyrian threat in 700 BC and only fell to the Babylonians in 597 and 587. The inhabitants were likewise deported to Babylon, but were allowed to return c. 530 BC, though not all took this opportunity afforded by the liberal policy of the new Persian rulers of Babylon. During the Babylonian exile the fervour of their devotion to Yahweh was very much increased and purified. To the returning exiles the inhabitants of the northern province were anathema, impure in race and religion. The moral in the parable of the man who fell among robbers (Luke 10: 30-37) is that the man deserving commendation is a Samaritan, one of the despised inhabitants of the northern province, whose behaviour was in such contrast to that of the orthodox Jews.

With this background, the reaction of the south and north to the spread of Hellenisation was entirely different. In the north it was accepted readily, and towns of Hellenistic type appear. The Jews of Jerusalem opposed it bitterly, and a climax was reached when Antiochus IV Epiphanes attempted in 167 BC to replace the worship of Yahweh by that of Olympian Zeus. The resultant Maccabean revolt was so successful that the small nucleus of Judea became virtually an independent Jewish state.

The Palestine of the time of the New Testament was essentially that created by Herod the Great. Herod was half Jewish, half Idumean, and by highly successful intrigues and with the backing of Rome he established himself as the heir of the Maccabean kings, and very considerably extended their kingdom. Herod was a great admirer of Rome and particularly of Augustus. He set himself to turn his towns into places worthy of the Roman Empire. They were not, of course, like Roman towns in the west, because they had a background which was either Hellenistic or Semitic, upon which Roman features were grafted.

The two places that provide the best archaeological evidence of Herod's building activities are Samaria and Jerusalem, and they emphasize the contrast in background of the north and the south. As early as about 300 BC Hellenistic-type buildings are found at

Samaria, and most of the domestic pottery used during the last centuries BC was imported from Greek lands or consisted of local copies of these imports. The inhabitants of Samaria took no part in the struggles of the Maccabean rulers of Jerusalem against the Hellenistic rulers of Syria, but the powers of the Maccabees had grown to such an extent that John Hyrcanus destroyed the city in 107 BC. It was rebuilt *c.* 60 BC, and remained throughout a town with a culture found widespread in the eastern Hellenistic world.

The inhabitants of Samaria, therefore, found nothing alien in Herod's conception of what an important town should look like, for Roman-style buildings grew naturally out of the Hellenistic buildings of the East. His aim was to provide the town with the public buildings suitable to its status. Two were of outstanding importance. One was a Temple of Augustus, classical in plan, and planted on the summit of the hill with a large courtyard to its

87 **Plan of the Roman buildings at Samaria.**
1 **Roman city wall;** 2 **West gate;**
3 **Street of Columns;** 4 **Shops;**
5 **Theatre;** 6 **Temple of Kore;**
9-10 **Forecourt and Temple of Augustus;** 13 **Basilica;** 14 **Forum;**
15 **Paved street;** 16 **Aqueduct;**
17 **Stadium**

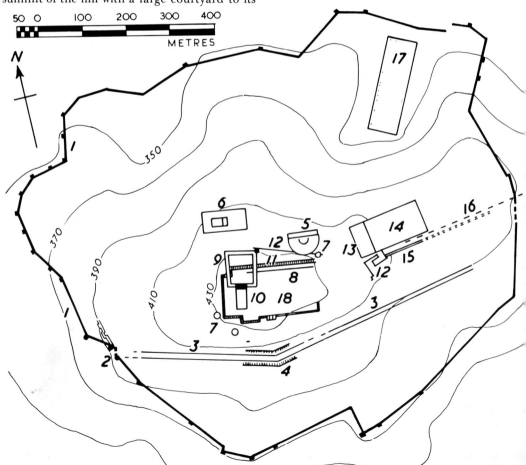

orth. It was founded on the platform which ad been created for the palace and royal uarter of the Israelite kings, but since that did ot provide sufficient space, a further great latform was built out to the north. A con-iderable part of a large stone statue of ugustus was found in the excavations of 908-10. The next most important building /as the typical civic centre of a Roman town, he Forum and Basilica, constructed to the east f the royal quarter on a level stretch that equired only a minimum of platform con-truction. To this building an aqueduct ,400 m. long brought water from a spring on he adjacent hill, which crossed the valley on a ridge 50 m. high (87).

A Roman city also required buildings for ntertainment. One such that was certainly of he Herodian period was a stadium for athletic ports on the lower slopes of the hill. At a later ime there was a theatre, of classical Roman orm, just below the summit of the hill, and it is ery likely that a Herodian theatre lies beneath .

There was at least one other temple of lassical type, probably at first dedicated to sis, though later superseded by one dedicated o the Kore. No doubt there were numerous ther temples and public buildings in the large rea of the Roman city not yet excavated.

Herod was therefore able to build at Samaria town which would have met with the ap-roval of his Roman friends. He changed its ame to Sebastia, the Greek equivalent of ugusta, in honour of his patron. Caesarea, gain named after the Roman Emperor, was a ompletely new creation out of an obscure ishing village. Little of the Herodian town ere is yet known, but its theatre and hippo-lrome would have had their origin in this eriod. Over most of Galilee, fragments such as he theatre at Bethshan remind us that the urban culture in New Testament times was Hellenistic-Roman, though the villages would probably have been simple and unsophistica-ed.

In the south, and especially in Jerusalem, the position was very different. Herod had to move very cautiously here in any attempts at moder-nisation. The fiercely xenophobic worshippers of Yahweh had, under the Maccabean rulers, saved themselves from absorption into the Hellenistic Empire of the Seleucids, and they would allow no later ruler to alter the character of their religion and their city.

The Jerusalem to which Herod succeeded had few pretensions to architectural distinc-tion. Such fragments of buildings as excava-tions have revealed are constructed for the most part in only roughly trimmed stones. The town walls of the Maccabean rulers have a certain massive strength, with stones with wide bosses and dressed margins, but if there were any other buildings in such a style, they have not survived. The city, however, had grown con-siderably from the small area, including only a part of the city destroyed in 587 BC, which was all that Nehemiah found necessary to defend in 440 BC. It now certainly included the northern summit of the western ridge, where Macca-bean-style masonry underlies Herodian struc-tures at the site of the present Citadel. There are many difficulties in establishing the exact plan of Maccabean Jerusalem, but the balance of evidence suggests a reasonable plan (88).

Herod's contribution to the appearance of Jerusalem was in buildings of much better architectural style. There had been no high-class masonry in Jerusalem since the time of Solomon. Of the Solomonic masonry nothing survives, but fortunately enough of the time of Herod is still visible to give an idea of what Jerusalem of the period of the Gospels looked like. An even better idea of a complete building of the period is given by the walls enclosing the Haram el Khalil or sanctuary of Abraham at Hebron, within which lie the traditional sites of the tombs of the Patriarchs.

Herod's major undertaking at Jerusalem was the rebuilding of the Temple. The rebuilding by Zerubbabel in 515 BC was carried out with slender resources and its appearance evoked sad comparisons from those who had known the earlier Temple; since then it had suffered many vicissitudes. Herod's desire to build some-thing more worthy of Jerusalem and of his own ambitions was justified. The Jewish historian, Flavius Josephus, writing after the destruction of Jerusalem by Titus in AD 70, but remember-ing it as it was early in the first century AD, describes it in ecstatic terms. Absolutely noth-ing survives of the Temple built by Herod

88 Plan of Maccabean Jerusalem

89 Typical Herodian masonry in
the western platform wall of the
rebuilt Temple

which Josephus remembered, for the platform
on which it stood is now occupied by the
Moslem sanctuary of the Dome of the Rock,
architecturally a very worthy successor. Archaeology can, however, recreate something of the
appearance of the Temple as one approached
it from the south, for much of the wall supporting the platform is Herodian work.

The distinctive feature of Herodian construction is the masonry. As previously mentioned, between Solomon's buildings of c. 960
BC and those of the time of Herod in the last
third of the first century BC, excavations in

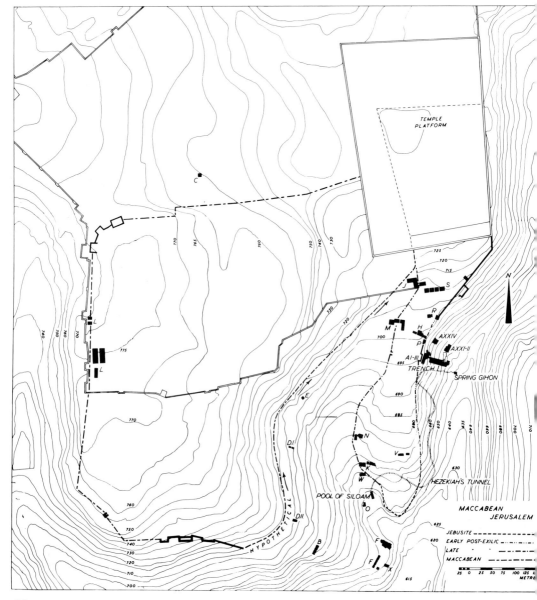

Jerusalem have produced no evidence of high-class masonry. The vernacular building style was based on the use of fairly rough blocks. It is tempting to believe that Herod, like Solomon, drew upon the resources of areas, probably the Lebanon, where there was a technique in architecture and in masonry which was superior to that in Judah. In fact, the immediately recognisable Herodian masonry (89) cannot be exactly paralleled. One cannot say that Herod brought masons from any one source, although the evidence may come to light one day. At the present stage, all that can be said is that the masonry techniques provide the foundation for the refurbishing of the Jerusalem of the New Testament.

The start of an archaeological appraisement of the appearance of Jerusalem in the period of the Gospels must concentrate on the structural features of the Temple platform. The archaeological evidence is absolutely clear. The joint between the Herodian masonry and the corner of the earlier platform (89) has already been described (pp. 53-4). This straight joint is seen 32.72 m. north from the south-east angle of the Temple platform, and from this point right

along the south face of the platform and up the western side for a distance of at least 185 m. Herodian masonry can be seen (89 and 90). At the south-east corner it still survives to *c.* 40 m. above the rock upon which the wall was founded. The platform, which Josephus describes as doubling the size of the Temple area, thus added 30 m. at the south end and probably nearly 200 m. along the west side. Most of these extended walls must have supported a fill of earth and stones, but along the south side, beneath the Royal Cloister, there were subterranean rooms with roofs supported on arches, at base Herodian in structure, which are today shown (only to persevering visitors) as 'Solomon's Stables'.

The whole appearance of the southern and south-western part of the Temple platform has been changed by recent excavations under the direction of Professor Mazar of the Hebrew University. He has exposed the paved street, found by Warren in 1867, running down the slope of the central valley along the west wall of the platform. From the south-west angle he has traced a connecting street climbing up along the south wall to reach the rock surface of the ridge upon which the platform is based. There, two gateways, the Double Gate and the Triple Gate, can be seen, rebuilt and now blocked, which led to passages sloping up to the interior surface of the Temple courtyard. Outside these entrances was found evidence of monumental steps leading up from the south. As seen today they are almost entirely reconstruction, but they give an impression of the lay-out.

Just north of the south-west angle there survives the spring of an arch which clearly carried a bridge westward from the Temple. This has long been known as Robinson's Arch, recalling its discovery by Edward Robinson early in the nineteenth century, and was for long rather romantically visible beneath scrub and cactus bushes. Now it is fully revealed (90), high in the air. Professor Mazar has shown that the passage from it connected with a staircase leading up from the south. He does not believe that it formed part of a complete bridge across the central valley. The negative evidence for this was not proved, but the positive structural evidence of a branch to the south is clear.

91 Reconstruction drawing of the south-west corner of the Temple platform at Jerusalem (*after* Mazar)

Whether or not Robinson's Arch was connected with a viaduct to the western hill, connections with the western hill were necessary, and Josephus describes the gates to the west from the Temple, though not so clearly as to answer all queries. Reference has already been made to the evidence for the inclusion of the western ridge within the city in the Maccabean period. Evidence for Herodian structures there is still visible, for at the present Citadel, on the right as one comes in through the Jaffa Gate, the lower courses of the so-called Tower of David are of Herodian masonry. This tower is part of Herod's palace, and can be identified as the tower Phasael, one of the three described by Josephus. The rest of the palace lay to the south, and may have covered much of the south-western sector of the present Old City, but little more than fragments have survived of retaining walls supporting the terrace upon which stood the buildings, gardens, pavilions and canals described by Josephus.

Of the Jerusalem that Jesus knew, therefore, we have two fixed points, high points in every sense of the word, the great artificial Temple platform to the east, and a fragment of Herod's palace on the higher hill to the west. In between, the appearance of the city may not have been all that different from the view today. The difference is that in the early first century AD the dip towards the central valley was much greater. As will be seen, the main levelling-up came with the lay-out of Aelia Capitolina in the second century AD.

Excavations carried out in the past ten years on the western ridge, beneath the Jewish Quarter destroyed in the fighting in 1948, have begun to give a picture of the houses of Jerusalem of the period of the Gospels. Most belong to the first century AD, forming part of the ruins of the city destroyed by Titus in AD 70. One house, however, belongs to the period of Herod the Great, for it was buried by a street of a new lay-out of the city at the beginning of the

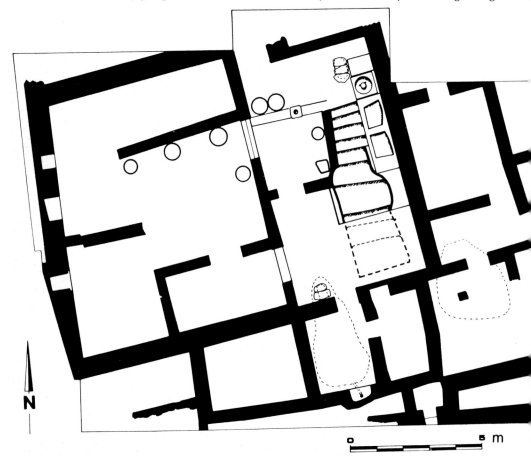

N

0   5 m

irst century AD (92). It shows that the houses ndicate wealth and comfort, at least in this irea, which had a favoured position looking owards the Temple. The house covered an irea of some 200 square metres, with rooms irranged round a central courtyard. Beneath he courtyard were large cisterns, for down to he period of the Mandate householders had to preserve all rainwater to be sure of an adequate vater supply. In cupboards in the walls were iumerous pottery vessels, with fine tableware of Eastern sigillata, a ware finished with a beautiful red glaze. Large jars with Latin tamps show, rather surprisingly, that the inhabitants of Jerusalem drank wine imported rom Italy. The actual masonry of the walls of he house, however, was not impressive, for the valls were constructed mainly of untrimmed stones, with the faces finished in plaster. It is interesting that this indigenous masonry style vas still used in private houses beside the new style in public buildings.

The houses destroyed in AD 70 showed similar signs of wealth, and had considerably more architectural pretensions, with walls built of ashlar and wall-plaster painted with architectural motifs, as at Pompeii, and mosaic floors in geometric patterns. Houses like this must have seemed very impressive to Jesus' disciples, simple peasants from Galilee.

It is only since the excavations directed by Professor Yigael Yadin between 1963 and 1965 that another of the great Herodian structures has been revealed. This is the incredible fortress-palace of Masada, situated high on a mountain overlooking the south end of the Dead Sea. The drama of the siege of the band of Jewish Zealots by the Romans, whose encircling camps and walls are still visible (93), and the culminating tragedy of the suicide of the defenders in AD 73 is tremendous. There is also a drama in the conversion by Herod of this most inaccessible mountain top into a site of palaces, administrative quarters and store-

92 Plan of a house of the Herodian period in Jerusalem (after Avigad)

93 Part of Herod's palace built on massive retaining walls at the north end of Masada. On the plain below can be seen the rectangular outline of a Roman siege camp

rooms. It seems incredible that such a civilised and cosmopolitan person as Herod should wish to retire to such a remote place. He may have had good reason for wanting a place of refuge there, but the magnificence of the buildings far exceeds the needs of such a refuge.

At Masada, even Herod could not work with the beautiful ashlars of his buildings in Jerusalem. Instead, walls constructed of soft local stone were covered with plaster and the surface painted in imitation marble panels (95), and the drums making up the Corinthian style columns were plastered and grooved to make them look like monoliths (94). One Corinthian capital was found on which the gold paint on the plaster was still preserved. These features were found in the magnificent and very private palace at the northern tip of the mountain, which had to be supported by enormous terrace walls to provide sufficient building space. They were also found in a bath house, which had all the features of such buildings throughout the Roman Empire. Beside all these features showing Herod's attachment to Rome were found a synagogue and a ritual bath for the Jewish members of his household.

Other examples of the Roman veneer that Herod the Great gave to the relatively simple urban and village landscape which is the background of New Testament are to be seen at Herodium and Jericho. At Herodium, designed as a fortress-palace and as his burial place, a mountain-top near Bethlehem was made additionally impressive by an enormous artificial cone of earth and stone visible for miles

94 Detail of fluted columns of Herod's palace building at Masada

95 Column bases on which stucco imitating the veining of marble is still preserved at Masada

round, and within the ramparts so construc-
ed were palace suites and a bath house similar
o those at Masada. At Jericho, Herod built
himself a Roman villa terraced up the sides of
he Wadi Qelt, which is so essentially Roman
hat the walls supporting the terrace and surrounding the sunk garden, swimming pool and
other features are constructed in *opus reticula-
um*, a technique typical of the Augustan
period in Italy, and rarely found elsewhere in
he Empire.

This Roman veneer over the culture of
Palestine of the first century AD forms the
greater part of the illustration provided by
archaeology of the life of the period. Only
rarely is evidence found of the religious background. The outstanding exception has been
the discovery of the Dead Sea Scrolls and of the
abode of the community to which they had
belonged.

The story of the accidental find in 1947 of
the first scrolls in a cave is well-known. The
cave is one of many in the cliffs at the base of
the mountains of Judah, fringing the north-
west end of the Dead Sea. Fragments of manuscripts were found in many of them. On a
plateau at the base of the cliffs, slightly above
the narrow plain along the shore, are the ruins
of a monastery (96). The ruins had been known
for a long time, but it was the possibility that
they had a connection with the scrolls that led
to their excavation between 1951 and 1956 by
Père Roland de Vaux. The buildings did in
fact prove to be the home of the community to
the library of which the scrolls had belonged.

The site was first occupied during the period
of the monarchy of Judah, down to the Babylonian destruction at the beginning of the sixth
century BC. The only important part of the
buildings of this period to be re-used by the
monastic community which settled there in the
Maccabean period was a great cistern into
which the winter torrents down the cliffs were
channelled. To this, many other cisterns were
added, for this winter rainfall was the only
source of water on the site.

This first monastic establishment was succeeded about 100 BC by a second, of which the
details could be traced more clearly (97). The
nucleus of the building was a roughly square
complex dominated by a tower (A) at the

96 Air view of the ruins of the
monastery of Qumran

97 Plan of the monastery of
Qumran (*after* de Vaux)

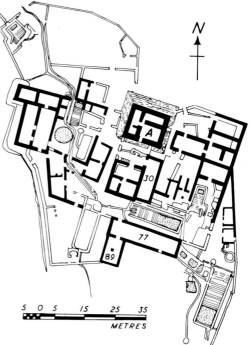

north-west corner. This was entered only at first floor level, with an approach by a wooden staircase, and its defensive character is evident. The rest of the complex consisted of courtyards and large rooms. To its south lay the most important of the public rooms, with a finely plastered floor, which can be recognised as a Place of Assembly (98). It was certainly also a dining room, for in an annex (plan, 89) were discovered stacks of table ware. That the meals may on occasion have had a ceremonial element is suggested by a multitude of small deposits of animal bones, buried when the flesh had been removed; the bones of animals eaten at these meals apparently could not just be thrown away.

The buildings outside this main block had a service nature, stores, stables, workshops and a potter's establishment. It can be very clearly deduced that the community was numerous, requiring a most elaborate canalisation of rain water from the cliffs into many cisterns, and requiring highly developed services. It is certainly a communal establishment, but the members of the community did not in fact live there, for there is no sign of any living quarters. It is possible that they lived mainly in the caves in the adjacent cliff face.

The buildings of this period were destroyed by a severe earthquake in 31 BC, which was followed by a fire. Thereafter there was a period of abandonment. The re-occupation can be fixed to the reign of Herod Archelaus, 4 BC-AD 6, and the restoration was certainly the work of the same community. Some buildings required strengthening. The tower A, was surrounded by a supporting buttressing wall. Some cisterns were so badly cracked that they went out of use. The debris in some rooms was so thick that it was simply sealed by a new floor at a higher level; a striking instance of this was the pantry, in which was found the stacked table ware of the earlier period. But the use of the rooms in general remained the same, and the remains of ceremonial meals continued to be buried in small pits.

This restoration at about the beginning of the first century AD represents the last stage of the life of the community. From its ruins the excavators were able to recover a remarkable amount of evidence of the way of life of the

98 View of the Place of Assembly at Qumran, number 77 on the plan (fig. 97)

99 Restored plaster tables in the North Cloister of the monastery at Qumran

100 Storage jars for scrolls. The upper example, restored from fragments, was excavated at Qumran, and the lower, complete example was found with scrolls inside it in the caves nearby

inhabitants. The emphasis is on the self-sufficiency of the community, its pottery work-shops, its milling establishment and other workshops. Most interesting of all is the find, in room 30, of plaster-covered benches and tables (99). These had fallen from an upper storey, and there can be very little doubt that this was the *scriptorium* where the scrolls were written. The connection of the scrolls with the building is made abundantly clear by the find in it of a storage jar identical with those in which the scrolls in the caves were stored, purpose-made in the pottery work-shops of the establishment (100). Moreover, Cave IV, the most prolific source of finds of manuscripts after the first one, was in the plateau upon which the buildings stood.

The Qumran buildings were destroyed in June AD 68 by the Romans in the course of their suppression of the First Revolt of the Jews. As the centre of a community, it ceased to exist, and its next stage is merely that of a minor Roman military post. The scrolls deposited in the caves, as storage places or to hide them against the imminent threat from the Romans, therefore can be dated as earlier than AD 68. Naturally, however, the library of the community contained many earlier documents, some as early as the third century BC.

The monastery and its library belonged to one of the ascetic sects of the Jews at this period. It is generally accepted that the community belonged to the sect of the Essenes, of which John the Baptist was probably a member. The importance of the scrolls for literary scholars and theologians is enormous, since they show the background of the text of the books of the Old Testament at a stage when present canonical form was being established. The importance to the historian, and also for the theologian, is that they provide evidence of the Jewish religion and culture to set against the veneer of Roman civilisation of the Herodian period.

This veneer of Roman civilisation and the unique evidence of the underlying Jewish culture provides the archaeological background for the period of the New Testament. In the main, very little material evidence of the Gospel story can be expected to survive. Claims that the house of Peter has been found at

Capernaum, based on the find in it of a fish-hook, must be regarded with some scepticism. The main question which has for many years been attracting the attention of archaeologists in Jerusalem is the authenticity of the site of Calvary and the Holy Sepulchre. Today, the Church of the Holy Sepulchre (104) is claimed to cover both sites.

In the nineteenth century, when critical discussion began to be concentrated on the problem, it was natural that many found difficulties in accepting this site as authentic. At that time the Old City of Jerusalem was accepted as the only Jerusalem, the city of David and Solomon and all their successors. The Church of the Holy Sepulchre lies in its heart (101), yet all the Biblical evidence points to Calvary and the Sepulchre being outside the walls. The present site is that on which Constantine the Great in AD 326-7, with the assistance of his mother the Empress Helena, constructed two buildings, one to enclose the sites identified as the Tomb and Golgotha, the second a great Basilica to the east. The site had been occupied by a Temple of Aphrodite, which Helena was told, on the basis of the traditions preserved by the Christian community in Jerusalem, covered the sacred sites. Since at the time of Helena the place was already in the heart of the contemporary town, and would have seemed as unlikely to her as it does to us, it is not unreasonable to believe that she must have been given some convincing evidence.

The archaeologists and historians of the nineteenth century did not have the evidence that we possess today that the present outline of the Old City is basically derived from that of Aelia Capitolina, the Roman city built by Hadrian c. AD 135. In an endeavour to solve the difficulty, they sought for other possible sites for Golgotha. There are in the rocky slopes to the north of the present Old City a number of rock-cut tombs. Some may date from the period of the Jewish monarchy, others from the first centuries BC-AD. Claude Conder, one of the archaeologists who worked for the Palestine Exploration Fund, proposed an identification of one of them as the Holy Sepulchre, and this identification was enthusiastically accepted by General Gordon. One of the reasons claimed for the identification was that the rocky outline

of the hill resembled a skull. Such a claim ignores the fact that the shape is due largely to relatively modern quarrying. The Garden Tomb illustrates the sort of tomb that was in use at the time, and is a pleasant and reverently-tended site, but there is no scientific evidence to support the identification.

In order to understand where the site of the Crucifixion and Tomb may have been, it is necessary to establish the position of the north wall of Jerusalem in the first half of the first century AD. On this, archaeology has recently provided a considerable amount of evidence, though there is still controversy on some aspects.

The historical evidence comes from the description of Flavius Josephus, an excellent historian, a Jew, but a renegade to the Romans. The description is in connection with the capture of Jerusalem by the Romans under Titus in AD 70. He describes three north walls that had successively to be stormed. The first ran from the site of Herod the Great's palace on the western hill at the present Citadel across the valley to the western side of the Temple platform. It is probably Maccabean in origin. The third was the work of Herod Agrippa between AD 40-44, and is therefore later than the date of the Crucifixion. Excavations at the present Damascus Gate showed that the original gate, the plan of which the present gate follows, belongs to this wall. The excavation evidence of this is clear, though there is a rival school that believes a wall c. 300 m. further north is the wall of Herod Agrippa, in spite of excavation evidence to the contrary. It is, however, only the line of the second wall that is relevant to the problem of the site of the Crucifixion. This Josephus describes as running from the Gate Gennath on the old north wall, the first wall, to the Fortress Antonia at the north-west corner of the Temple platform. The problem is the position of the Gate Gennath. For long it was held that it was in the neighbourhood of the present Citadel, and it required considerable ingenuity to suggest a line that did not enclose the site of the Church of the Holy Sepulchre. Another suggestion, however, placed the Gate Gennath half-way along the first north wall from which a line to the north would lie to the east of the Church. Excavations, those of the

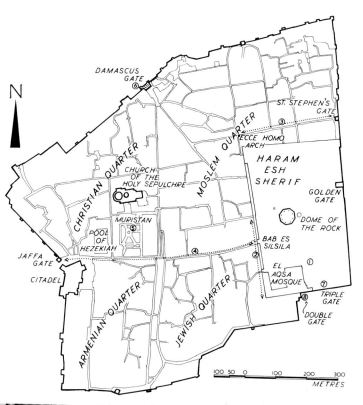

N

101 Map of the present Old City of Jerusalem showing the position of the Church of the Holy Sepulchre at its centre

102 Excavations in the Muristan to the south of the Church of the Holy Sepulchre showing, at the base, quarrying sealed by an Iron Age deposit level with the man's shoulder. Above him is fill of the first/second centuries AD

British School in the Muristan and of the German School beneath the Lutheran Church, proved that this was the correct alternative. Both excavations found that in this area, to the south of the Church, there was an enormous depth of artifical fill. At Site C in the British excavations, this was found to overlie a quarry of seventh century BC date (102). A quarry is almost certain to be outside the walls of the contemporary town. Above the seventh-century fill of that quarry there was no trace of occupation down to the period of the deep fill. The site remained outside the town until the period of the fill, which contains much debris from the destruction by Titus in AD 70, with a little material probably of early second century AD date. It belongs, in fact, to the great building operations associated with the construction of Aelia Capitolina by Hadrian. Since on this evidence Site C and the excavation area beneath the Lutheran Church were outside the city in the first century AD, the site of the Church of the Holy Sepulchre was also outside the walls (103). Archaeology therefore has shown that the site of the Church may be authentic, though it has not shown that this is

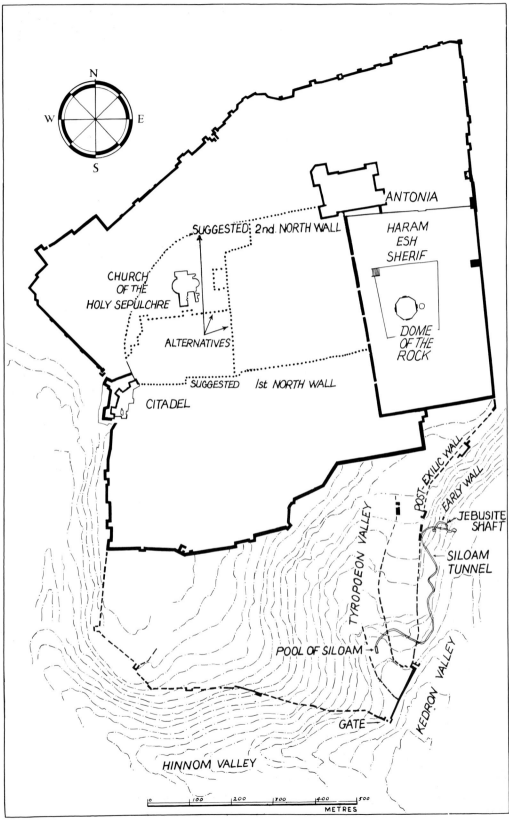

N
W E
S

SUGGESTED 2nd. NORTH WALL

ANTONIA

HARAM
ESH
SHERIF

CHURCH
OF THE
HOLY SEPULCHRE

ALTERNATIVES

DOME
OF THE
ROCK

SUGGESTED 1st NORTH WALL

CITADEL

POST-EXILIC WALL

EARLY WALL

JEBUSITE
SHAFT

SILOAM
TUNNEL

TYROPOEON VALLEY

POOL OF SILOAM

KEDRON VALLEY

GATE

HINNOM VALLEY

0   100   200   300   400   500
METRES

so and cannot do so. Here the tradition of the Christian community recounted to the Empress Helena must remain the basic evidence.

Jerusalem of the period of the Crucifixion and of the enlarged city of Herod Agrippa was utterly destroyed by the Romans under Titus in AD 70. The 1961-7 excavations in Old Testament Jerusalem, and the more recent excavations within the Old City, have everywhere uncovered evidence of the destruction. Almost more disastrous for the ancient city was its deliberate obliteration by the construction of Aelia Capitolina over the ruins in AD 135. The walls of Aelia are probably fairly closely represented by those built fourteen hundred years later by Suleiman the Magnificent, the present Old City. Earliest Jerusalem and much of Jerusalem of the monarchic and succeeding Maccabean period was left outside the walls, and suffered the fate of quarrying to provide building material for the new city. Within it, elevated areas were levelled down and depressions were filled in, of which the evidence in the area south of the Church of the Holy Sepulchre is an example. This levelling produced an area in which the basic contours, a slope from north to south and a central valley between the

Citadel to the west and the Temple platform to the east, are still visible, but much less accentuated than previously. On this was laid out a Roman city, of which the street plan is still reflected in that of the present Old City (101), and beneath which the Roman drains can still be traced.

This descendant of Aelia Capitolina is that in which the traditional places associated with the New Testament are shown today. Their identification with sites and events that took place in the Jerusalem obliterated by Titus has a foundation only in the tradition of pilgrims. Here archaeology can give little help, and such evidence as has emerged has been more negative than positive. This does not mean that many of the sites are not very impressive, for they are hallowed by centuries of tradition.

There are many areas in the interpretation of both the Old and New Testaments in which archaeology can offer no assistance. These sites and places traditionally associated with the events recorded in the Gospels are one category, for in the main these events are of a nature unlikely to leave material evidence. The contribution of archaeology can only be based on an interpretation of factual evidence preserved in the soil and in buildings. The interpretation of this evidence must take into account literary records of all sorts, including that of the Bible. To the Bible the material remains revealed and interpreted by archaeology provide a background. These chapters have attempted to describe present knowledge on this subject.

103 Plan of Jerusalem showing the suggested alternative lines for the north wall

104 The restored facade of the Church of the Holy Sepulchre

Bibliography

General

AHARONI, Y.
The Land of the Bible. London, 1966.

ALBRIGHT, W. F.
Archaeology of Palestine. Harmondsworth, 1949.

AVI-YONAH, M. Edit.
Encyclopedia of Archaeological Excavations in the Holy Land. London, 1975, 1976.

DE VAUX, R.
Histoire Ancienne d'Israël. Paris, 1971.

GLUECK, N.
Explorations in Eastern Palestine, I, II, III. N. Glueck, *Annual of the American Schools of Oriental Research* XIV, XV, XVIII-XIX. New Haven, 1934, 1935, 1939.

GRAY, J.
Archaeology and the Old Testament World. Edinburgh, 1962.

JOSEPHUS.
The Jewish War, translated by G. A. Williamson. Harmondsworth, 1959.

JOSEPHUS.
The Works of Flavius Josephus, translated by W. Wheston. Halifax, 1864.

KENYON, F. G.
The Bible and Archaeology. London, 1940.

KENYON, K. M.
Archaeology in the Holy Land. London, 3rd edition, 1969.

KENYON, K. M.
Royal Cities of the Old Testament. London, 1971.

KENYON, K. M.
Amorites and Canaanites. Scnweich Lectures 1963, London, 1966.

NOTH, M.
The History of Israel. London, 2nd English edition, 1960.

Sites

'AI
Les Fouilles de 'Ay (et Tell). Y. Marquet. Institut Francais d'Archéologie de Beyrouth, 1949.
'The 1964 'Ai (et Tell) Excavations', J. A. Callaway, in *Bulletin of the American Schools of Oriental Research* 178, 1965.
'The Significance of the Iron Age Village at 'Ai (et Tell)', J. A. Callaway, in *Proceedings of the Fifth World Congress of Jewish Studies.*

TELL 'AS
In 'Une Campagne de Fouilles à Khan Sheikhun, du Mesnil du Buisson', in *Syria* XIII.

BEERSHEBA
Beersheba I. Y. Aharoni. Tel Aviv, 1973.

TELL BEIT MIRSIM
Tell Beit Mirsim I, Ia, II, III. Annuals of the American Schools of Oriental Research XII, XIII, XVII, XXI-XXII. W. F. Albright. New Haven, 1932, 1933, 1938, 1943.

BETH-SHAN
I The Topography and History of Beth-shan. A. Rowe. Pennsylvania, 1930.
II The Four Canaanite Temples of Beth-shan A. Rowe. Pennsylvania, 1940.
The Iron Age at Beth-shan. F. W. James. Pennsylvania, 1966.

BRAK
'Excavations at T. Brak', M. E. L. Mallowan, in *Iraq* IX.

BUSEIRA
'Excavations at Buseira, Southern Jordan, Preliminary Reports', C. M. Bennett in *Levant* V, VI, VII, IX.

BYBLOS
Fouilles de Byblos I, II. M. Dunand, Paris 1926-32 and 1933-38.
'Byblos au Temps du Bronze Ancien et de la Conquête Amorite', M. Dunand in *Revue Biblique* LIX, 1959.

EBLA
Missione archeologica in Siria. Preliminary reports 1964, 1965, 1966, 1967-8. P. Matthiae et al, in *Instituto di Studi del Vicino Oriente-Università,* Rome, 1965-7, 1972.
'Ebla a l'Epoque d'Akkad: Archéologie et Histoire'. P. Matthiae in *Academie des Inscriptions et Belles-Lettres Compte Rendu,* 1976.

TELL EL-FAR'AH (N)
'Les Fouilles de Tell el-Far'ah près Naploux. 5th campagne', R. de Vaux in *Revue Biblique* LXII, 1955.

GEZER

The Excavations of Gezer I-III, R. A. S.
Macalister, London, 1912.
Gezer I, II (HUC), W. G. Dever, *et al.*
Jerusalem, 1970, 1974.
'Solomon's City Wall and Gate at Gezer',
Y. Yadin in *Israel Exploration Journal* 8,
1958.
'Further Excavations at Gezer, 1967-71',
W. G. Dever *et al*, in *Biblical Archaeologist*
XXXIV, 1971.
Review of *Gezer II* (HUC), K. M. Kenyon in
Palestine Exploration Quarterly 1977.

HAZOR

Hazor I, II and III-IV, Y. Yadin *et al.*
Jerusalem, 1958, 1960, 1961.
Hazor, Y. Yadin, Schweich Lectures 1970.
London, 1972.

HERODIUM

'L'Herodion di Giabal Fureidis', V. Corbo in
Liber Annuus XIII and XVII, 1962/3 and
1967.

JERICHO

Digging Up Jericho. K. M. Kenyon. London,
1957.
Excavations at Jericho I, II. K. M. Kenyon,
London, 1960, 1965.

JERICHO (ROMAN)

Excavations at New Testament Jericho.
J. L. Kelso. *Excavations at Herodian Jericho*.
J. B. Pritchard, *Annuals of the American
School of Oriental Research* XXIX-XXX,
1955, and XXXII-XXXIII, 1958.

JERUSALEM

Excavations at Jerusalem 1894-1897. F. G.
Bliss and A. C. Dickie, London, 1898.
Digging Up Jerusalem, K. M. Kenyon,
London, 1974.
*The Church of the Holy Sepulchre in
Jerusalem*, C. Coüasnon. Schweich Lectures
1972. London, 1974.
'New Evidence on Solomon's Temple', K. M.
Kenyon, in *Melanges de l'Université Saint
Joseph*, vol. XLVI, Beyrouth, 1970.
'L'Antonia d'Hérode le Grand et le Forum
Oriental d'Aelia Capitolina', P. Benoit, in
Harvard Theological Review 64, 1971.
*Archaeological Discoveries in the Jewish
Quarter of Jerusalem*. N. Avigad, Jerusalem,
1976.
Jerusalem Revealed. Y. Yadin, ed., Jerusalem,
1975.
'The Citadel, Jerusalem', C. N. Johns, in
*Quarterly of the Department of Antiquities of
Palestine* XIV.

'Où en est la question du "Troisième Mur"?',
P. Benoit, in *Studia Hierosolymitana*, Part I
of no. 22 in *Studium Biblicum Franciscanum*,
1976.

LACHISH

I The Lachish Letters, H. Torczyner, *et al.*
London, 1938.
II The Fosse Temple, O. Tufnell, C. H. Inge,
G. L. Harding. London, 1940.

MARI

Mission archéologique de Mari, II, Le Palais,
A. Parrot, *et al.* Institut Français
d'Archéologie de Beyrouth LXVIII-LXX,
Paris, 1958-9.
'Mari', A. Malamat, in *Biblical Archaeology*,
XXXIV, 1971.

MASADA

Masada, Y. Yadin, London, 1966.

MEGIDDO

I Seasons of 1925-34. Strata I-V, R. S. Lamon
and G. M. Shipton. Chicago, 1939.
II Seasons of 1935-9. G. Loud. Chicago, 1948.
The Megiddo Water System. R. S. Lamon.
Chicago, 1935.
Megiddo Tombs. P. L. O. Guy and R. M.
Engberg. Chicago, 1938.
'The Middle and Late Bronze Age Strata at
Megiddo', K. M. Kenyon in *Levant* I, 1969.
'New Light on Solomon's Megiddo', Y. Yadin
in *Biblical Archaeologist* XXIII, 1960.
'Megiddo of the Kings of Israel', Y. Yadin,
Biblical Archaeologist XXXIII, 1970. *See
also: Hazor*, Schweich Lectures, Y. Yadin.

NIMRUD

Nimrud and its Remains, M. E. L. Mallowan.
London, 1966.

QATNA

'Les Ruines d'el-Mishrifé au Nord-Est de
Homs (l'Emèse)', le Comte du Mesnil du
Buisson, in *Syria* VII-IX.

QUMRAN

*L'Archéologie et les Manuscrits de la Mer
Morte.* R. de Vaux. Schweich Lectures 1959.
London, 1961.

RAS SHAMRA

Ugaritica II, IV. C. F. A. Schaeffer, Paris,
1949, 1962.

SAMARIA

Samaria-Sebaste 1: The Buildings. J. W.
Crowfoot, K. M. Kenyon, E. L. Sukenik.
London, 1942.
—2: *Early Ivories from Samaria*, J. W. and
G. M. Crowfoot. London, 1938.
—3: *The Objects*, J. W. Crowfoot, G. M.
Crowfoot, K. M. Kenyon. London, 1957.

Acknowledgements

The author and publishers are grateful to the following institutions and individuals for permission to reproduce the material acknowledged. All other illustrations are provided by the author.

Beersheba:
By permission of the Institute of Archaeology, Tel Aviv University.

Beth-shan:
From *Four Temples of Beth-shan*, by permission of the University Museum, Philadelphia.

Brak:
Iraq IX pl. XXXI, by permission of Sir Max Mallowan.

Ebla:
Italian Archaeological Mission to Syria of the University of Rome, by permission of Professor Paulo Matthiae.

Gezer:
(masonry of gateway)
By permission of the Palestine Exploration Fund, 2 Hinde Mews, Marylebone Lane, London, W.1.

Gezer:
(view of gate)
Hebrew Union College, Biblical and Archaeological School in Jerusalem, by permission of Dr W. G. Dever.

Hazor:
The James A. de Rothschild Expedition at Hazor, by permission of Professor Y. Yadin. Schweich Lectures, by permission of the British Academy.

Jericho:
Jericho Excavation Fund, c/o British School of Archaeology in Jerusalem, 2 Hinde Mews, Marylebone Lane, London, W.1.

Jerusalem:
Jerusalem Excavation Fund, c/o British School of Archaeology in Jerusalem, 2 Hinde Mews, Marylebone Lane, London, W.1.

Jerusalem:
(south-west angle of platform)
From *Jerusalem Revealed*, by permission of Professor B. Mazar.

Jerusalem:
(House of Herodian period) From catalogue of Israeli Museum, by permission of Professor N. Avigad.

Jerusalem:
Holy Sepulchre. By permission of the Bureau Technique Commun pour les travaux de restauration du Saint Sepulchre.

Lachish:
By permission of the Wellcome Trust, and the Trustees of the British Museum.

Mari:
By permission of Professor A. Parrot.

Masada:
Israel Exploration Society, by permission of Professor Y. Yadin and the Israel Government Tourist Office.

Megiddo:
By permission of the Oriental Institute, University of Chicago.

Nimrud:
From *Nimrud and its Remains*, by permission of Sir Max Mallowan.

Qumran:
(Plans) By permission of the École Biblique et Archéologique de St. Etienne, Jerusalem.
(De Vaux, Schweich Lectures Pl. XXIa, XXIb) By permission of the Rockefeller Museum, Jerusalem.
(De Vaux, Schweich Lectures Pl. IXa) By permission of L'Abbé Jean Starcky.
(Air view) Pictorial Archive (Near Eastern History), P.O. Box 19823, Jerusalem. Dr R. Cleave.

Ras Shamra:
Mission de Ras Shamra, by permission of Professor C. F. A. Schaeffer.

Samaria:
By permission of the Palestine Exploration Fund.

Sendchirli:
By permission of Dr David Ussishkin after *I.E.J.* 16-3.

Tell el Fariah:
Pictorial Archive (Near Eastern History). Dr R. Cleave.

Index